A former Sheffield steel worker and trade union convenor, Mick Drewry graduated from Sheffield Hallam University in 1997. He worked as a volunteer and then paid worker for a local community group before moving to Barnsley Council as a community development worker in 2002. Progressing to senior support worker, he took early retirement in 2010. *Infantrymen* is his fifth publication and fourth as author.

This book is dedicated to the Pridmore family, past and present.

Mick Drewry

INFANTRYMEN

The Story of the Pridmore Brothers –
Four Sheffield Brothers Killed in
the Great War 1914-1918

AUSTIN MACAULEY PUBLISHERS®
LONDON * CAMBRIDGE * NEW YORK * SHARJAH

All of the events in this memoir are true to the best of author's memory. The views expressed in this memoir are solely those of the author.

A CIP catalogue record for this title is available from the British Library.

ISBN 9781037116520 (Paperback)
ISBN 9781037116537 (ePub e-book)

www.austinmacauley.com

First Published 2026
Austin Macauley Publishers Ltd®
1 Canada Square
Canary Wharf
London
E14 5AA

Acknowledgements

All of my previous books have required input from other parties, for which I have been most grateful, and this one is no exception. The subject matter has required essential input from members of the Pridmore family, and I much appreciate the information and photographs provided by them. I am especially grateful to Ben Pridmore, whose extensive research into his line of the Pridmore family history formed the foundations for Chapter 1.

I would also like to thank other members of the extended Pridmore family: Alan Pridmore, John Pridmore, brothers Ray and Paul Pridmore, Barbara Bobrowicz, Sue Rydiard, Sue Mansell, Maureen Ashe and the late Roy Stacey for their contributions.

My research has been aided by my second cousin, David Williamson, who has contributed much information from research he undertook on my behalf. Similarly, Chris Hobbs, who has helped me with my research for previous books, has again provided me with invaluable historical research from his own sources.

I regret that two of my sources of inspiration are no longer with us, but I won't forget their contribution to my decision to finally write this book and the essential information that they provided: the late George Horner and the late Jeff Burdett.

I would also like to thank Ken Wild of the Friends of Burngreave Chapel and Cemetery group for his kind permission to use the group's cemetery map and for information relating to Pridmore grave locations.

I am most grateful to Cllr Denise Fox of Sheffield City Council, and to Alexa Stott of East Midland Railways, for making the arrangements for the installation of the Pridmore brothers' plaque at Sheffield Midland Station, and the four anonymous former Master Cutlers who generously paid for it.

Finally, and as ever, my writing is in need of scrutiny and, once more, my work has been proofread by my daughter, Kathryn Hewson.

Thank you all!
Mick Drewry, 2025

Table of Contents

Preface

My journey towards writing this, my fourth book, began long before I ever contemplated writing the first. In fact, it started before I could write at all.

As a young lad, I often visited my grandad, who lived on Broughton Road, within easy walking distance of our cottage on Bradfield Road, Owlerton. I was just six years old when my grandma Pridmore passed away, and I spent many hours with Grandad Pridmore in the early evenings whilst my mum was at work at Bassett's confectioners, just below Broughton Road on Beulah Road, and at weekends.

I often stopped for tea or Sunday dinner, and on one such occasion I had him in stitches when he asked me what part of the chicken I would like. 'A back leg, please, Grandad,' I told him, something he would never forget and would often remind me of.

Grandad didn't have a television and we spent time listening to the radio together; I particularly remember programmes like *The Goon Show, The Clitheroe Kid, Sing Something Simple* and religiously listening to the football results at Saturday tea time so as to check his football pools. If Sheffield Wednesday were at home, we could hear the roar of the crowd and knew when the Owls had scored.

Of course, I would soon get bored with the radio, and I would venture into the cupboard between the fireplace and the cellar door, which contained a number of biscuit tins full of all sorts of curiosities that I would rummage through until I found something of interest to play with.

One tin was full of pencils, crayons and pens that I would use to draw with. I had a natural talent for drawing and spent hours at the table drawing whatever interested me at the time: football, speedway, animals, locomotives, ships and aeroplanes.

Had I not been failed by the education system, I may well have gone on to art college, as my dad hoped, instead of joining the multitude of factory fodder that comprehensive schools turned out at the time, and ending up in the steel industry.

Now I turn back to the subject matter, for one of the tins in the cupboard was different to the others. It was much smaller and made of brass, with the profile of a young lady in the centre flanked by two letter Ms. Around the hinged tin lid was an embossed decorated border with roundels at each corner and one either side of the centre, each bearing the name of a country: Belgium, France, Servia, Russia, Japan and Montenegro. Top centre was the legend *Imperium Britannicum*, and across the bottom, *Christmas 1914*, flanked by the bow and stern of a battleship.

Most readers will know that this is a Princess Mary Christmas gift box that was distributed to all members of the armed forces at Christmas 1914 during the First World War.

Inside this tin was something special. It contained six medals, complete with ribbons; two sets of First World War medals. I marvelled at these medals, as my grandad had told me that one trio belonged to his dad, who was killed in the War. He also showed me the 'Big Penny' memorial plaque bearing the name John Thomas Pridmore. The other trio belonged to his stepfather, as his mother later re-married. The Princess Mary tin would have been presented to his stepfather, as John Thomas was killed in action in October 1914 and didn't see Christmas.

So, I had known from an early age that my great-grandfather had been killed in the First World War and, although it felt special on a personal level, I didn't think it would be of great interest to anybody else. After all, many thousands of people were killed in the First World War and many more in the Second World War, which was within recent memory and more often talked about.

As I grew up, like a lot of young lads, I developed an interest in the Wars, and I started collecting memorabilia from many of the second-hand shops that existed in those days: cap badges, medals, insignia, etc., which could be picked up for a few bob. I spent many hours constructing Airfix kits and reading war magazines, including collecting the full sets of Purnell's histories of the two World Wars.

When I started work, I collected bayonets, swords and helmets, which decorated my bedroom. I inherited my great-grandad's medals and memorial plaque and, although I tried to find out more about his Army service, I found little more than the whereabouts he was likely to have been killed. There was no significant battle on the date that he was killed, so my knowledge of John Thomas Pridmore's active service remained scant.

That changed in 2002.

By 2002, I had long left the steel industry, thanks to the Tory government's de-industrialisation and anti-trade union policies, and had returned to education, gaining a degree. In November that year, I started employment with Barnsley Council, working as a Community Development Worker in the Barnsley Dearne area (Thurnscoe, Goldthorpe and Bolton-upon-Dearne), supporting the Barnsley Dearne Community Partnership (BDCP), an umbrella organisation consisting of local community groups.

The Chair of BDCP was a retired college lecturer called George Horner,[1] who took a great interest in the military and was a mind of information from years of research. So intense was his interest that, for his annual holidays, he and his wife would tow a caravan around France, visiting war cemeteries and battlefield sites. He had collected a library of war material and had undertaken much research over the years.

I mentioned my great-grandfather to him one day and, on giving him as much information as I had, he said he would find out as much as he could for me. It wasn't long before he came back to me with maps of the action that my great-grandfather's battalion had been involved in around the date that he was killed. He had also consulted the Commonwealth War Graves Commission website and found the cemetery where he is commemorated (there is no gravestone, as he was buried where he fell), and he would make a point of visiting this cemetery on his next holiday and get me a photograph of the panel that his name appears.

True to his word, George returned from his holiday with photographs of the Le Touret Memorial, Pas-de–Calais, and of Panel 31 bearing the name *Pridmore J T*. Then came an astonishing revelation, as George pointed out to me on the photograph of the panel, under the 'Serjeant' heading, the name *Pridmore A E*! George had done a search for this sergeant and found that Arthur Edward was, as he suspected, John Thomas's brother. But that was not all.

On consulting the *De Ruvigny's Roll of Honour,*[2] George had found two more of my great-grandfather's brothers: Albert and George Harry. As the reader

---

[1] Sadly, George Horner passed away in February 2025.

[2] Originally published in five volumes, *Marquis De Ruvigny's Roll of Honour* features biographies of over 26,000 Army, Navy and Air Force men, both officers and other ranks, killed in the First World War.

can imagine, I was completely gobsmacked at this revelation. Not only was my great-grandfather killed in the First World War, but also three of my great-uncles; four brothers who made the ultimate sacrifice for King and country.

Once the enormity of this information sank in, I thought that the Pridmore brothers deserved some recognition. I had taken an interest in local history on taking the Diploma course at Northern College, then as an undergraduate at Sheffield Hallam University; my degree was in Social & Cultural Studies. It was an interest that inspired me to eventually write books on the Great Sheffield Flood of 1864, the Sheffield Outrages and Sheffield riots, and I knew of no other Sheffield family to have suffered such loss in the First World War, or any war, for that matter.

I gathered as much information as I could and wrote letters to the local press relating the story of the Pridmore brothers, in the hope that someone with influence within local authority circles shared my enthusiasm for their recognition and would instigate some form of civic honour.

As we approached the centenary of the start of the War in 2014, I gave it another shot and wrote another piece for the *Sheffield Star Retro* supplement. Still no interest from Sheffield Council, but I was contacted by a writer for a new local magazine for the Broomhill, Crookes and Walkley area, entitled *Ten,* to comment on an article he had written on the Pridmore brothers to be included in the magazine's first issue. I was more than happy to help with this, as it would provide further coverage of the Pridmore brothers' story in the area where much of the family was living at the time of the War.

Determined to at least get a response from the Sheffield Council, I wrote directly to the cabinet member I thought would have such things within his remit. Months passed by, and not even an acknowledgement of my letter. Then, in the summer of 2023, I got an email from a council officer who informed me that my correspondence had been passed to Councillor Denise Fox, who represented local veterans, and that she was keen to do something. The Pridmore brothers' story would be discussed at an internal meeting in due course.

The outcome of that meeting was an idea for a plaque at a prominent site in the city. Following further internal discussions, a meeting was arranged between a senior council officer and members of the family.

On 16 August, three members of the wider Pridmore family, Ben Pridmore, Sue Rydiard, Sue Mansell, and I met with Paul Taylor, Chief Communications

Officer at Sheffield City Council, to discuss the proposed plaque at its proposed site: Sheffield Midland Station.

After further discussions and exchanges of information with various parties, a stainless steel plaque was to be unveiled at the station on Friday, 10 November, Armistice weekend. A programme for the event was put together, which included a uniformed military presence, banners and bugles. The Lord Mayor was to unveil the plaque along with the Deputy Lord Lieutenant, and I was included in the speeches.

Despite the Lord Mayor and Deputy Lord Lieutenant failing to arrive (apparently there was royalty in the area commemorating an elephant, which clashed, despite the lengthy organisation process), it was a wonderfully moving event and the people of Sheffield did the Pridmore brothers proud, with a tremendous turnout to honour them, along with over twenty members of the Pridmore family attending from as far away as Birmingham and Liverpool and points in between. It was a day I will never forget and one of those especially memorable days of my life.

Following the experience of pride and a sense of achievement engendered by the unveiling ceremony, I was inspired to take the Pridmore brothers' story to another level, for I do believe that they deserve more than a simple A4 plaque at the railway station. As I write this preface, I still have much research to undertake, piecing together the story of each of the four brother's journey. But, as with my previous books, I want to raise the profile of yet another understated aspect of Sheffield's history.

I hope I achieve my objective and that you enjoy reading the Pridmore brothers' story.

Introduction

The Great War, 1914–1918, took the lives of 6,000 Sheffield servicemen in combat on land, at sea and in the air. Families lost fathers, husbands and brothers, and in Sheffield, no family lost more than the Pridmore family, with four brothers making the ultimate sacrifice: John Thomas, Arthur Edward, Albert and George Harry. This is their story, and that of the Pridmore family.

Three of the four brothers were born in Sheffield, but their parents were of rural stock and had moved to the steel city from Northamptonshire in 1880 with the first two of their eventual thirteen children. John Thomas was the first to be born in Sheffield and the first to join the Army, serving in South Africa fighting the Boers. Arthur Edward soon followed him into the ranks, serving in the Mediterranean during the Second Boer War, and staying in the Army to become a recruiting sergeant. He was the first of the brothers to go to France in August 1914. John served his six years, then re-enlisted as the Great War began. John and Arthur served together in France and Flanders, and died within four days of each other in October 1914. Albert, the oldest of the four, didn't sign up until 1915 and was wounded in May 1917. He died from his wounds the following month at Bradford Hospital. George Harry was the youngest of the four, and he enlisted in January 1914. A keen soldier, he quickly gained promotion through the NCO hierarchy, being promoted to acting sergeant in the field, then recommended for a commission, also in the field, becoming a 2nd Lieutenant. George was killed in action at the end of August 1918, within weeks of the armistice.

We begin the brothers' journey by looking at the Pridmore family history, picking each of them up at their birth along the way, then following their lives as much as we can until they each made the fateful decision to join the British Army. We also discover how the Pridmore family grew after migrating to Sheffield, and how they experienced a new way of life that not simply benefitted their economic standing but took away as much, if not more, than it received in unfolding events.

Having moved to Sheffield in search of higher wages and better job security that the booming town offered, they also had to endure the effects of one of Britain's dirtiest towns on their health and wellbeing, with its overcrowded housing and insanitary conditions; a huge change to their previous rural existence. In particular, as we shall see, the impact of the town's high infant mortality rate, which persisted well into the 20th century.

We cannot know what the four fated brothers did on a day-to-day basis as they played their part in the *'war to end wars'*, but we can follow their battalions and get an understanding of the horrors of war that they would have faced and endured. We also get an informed look at the nature of the Great War from a soldier's viewpoint and an introduction to the brothers' comrades who also died along the way and alongside them.

Following each of the brothers' stories, we consider the possibility that history could have recorded not four but seven Pridmore brothers being killed in the Great War. Three of their other brothers enlisted during the War, two being wounded in it, the other not actually seeing action but just missing it whilst undergoing his initial training and then being sent to Mesopotamia after hostilities had ended: Wilfred, Oswald and Sidney. The other brother, Ernest, whilst not doing active service, certainly contributed invaluable work towards the War effort producing shells and armour plating in the steel works.

Not wanting to leave them out, I have also included a chapter on the three Pridmore sisters, born in succession to William and Sarah, following their first four sons and prior to their last six. Their story too is one of tragedy and sorrow.

To conclude the story of the four Pridmore brothers and their families, we consider the impact of their deaths on their widows and, for two of them, their children. How did their widows manage, having lost their husbands and the security of their income? What emotional impact did it have on them and their children? Again, we cannot know how they felt, but we can gain an understanding of what War widows experienced in general and the impact on children left fatherless by the War as we consider their story.

The final act of the Pridmore brothers' story is the overdue civic recognition of their sacrifice, more than a century after their deaths, with the unveiling of a stainless steel plaque to commemorate them at Sheffield Midland Station on

Friday 10 November 2023. Their sacrifice will now be remembered every year by the people of Sheffield at Remembrance time.

The stainless steel plaque at Sheffield Midland Railway Station

The Pridmore Family[3]

'They all seem to have individual personalities bursting from the dry records of births, marriages and death, so much so that I almost feel like I know them.'[4]

The story of the Pridmore brothers begins not in Sheffield but in the village of Bourn in Lincolnshire.[5] At Bourn in 1835, saddler and harness maker James Pridmore's eldest daughter, Jane, gave birth to an illegitimate baby girl who she named Eliza, probably after her mother, Elizabeth Pridmore (née Ward). There being no father to register on Eliza's birth certificate, she was given her mother's surname. It is likely that Jane and Eliza stayed with James and Elizabeth, and that she was supported by them until Jane was either able to find work or a husband. James, being a skilled craftsman, would have a good, steady income and would be able to support Jane and her baby, saving them from dire poverty and the workhouse. Jane may well have been able to help James with the more menial tasks, or perhaps she had learnt some of her father's skills.

---

[3] I am grateful to Ben Pridmore for sharing his family history research, which is my main source of information about the Pridmore family. Also, two more of my second cousins who I made contact with during my initial research: Maureen Ashe and the late Roy Stacey. See Appendix 7 for the Pridmore family tree.

[4] Ben Pridmore, from his blog on the Pridmore family.
See zoomy.blogspot.com/2011/03/census-day.html.

[5] Sometimes spelt *Bourne*.

Bourn Town Centre 1875

On 2 September 1838, Jane married labourer William Stapleton at Elton, Northamptonshire, and moved to Helpstone,[6] where she gave birth to a baby boy on 15 June 1839, who they named Abraham. William Stapleton died soon after, and in the 1841 census, 6-year-old Eliza Pridmore and 2-year-old Abraham Stapleton are living with their grandparents, James and Elizabeth Pridmore, at 115 Star Lane back in Bourn; the whereabouts of the widowed Jane Stapleton is unknown. It could be that she was in the village of Pickworth, Rutland,[7] where she later married 38-year-old farm labourer Thomas Fowler on Christmas Eve 1849. Jane and Thomas Fowler and the two children moved in with Thomas's 85-year-old father, John.

We know little of Eliza's life with the Stapletons or the Fowlers, other than when she was old enough, in 1850, she started work as a domestic servant at a large farm in the small village of Swinstead,[8] about 6 miles west of Bourn, owned by William Ward. It is possible that William Ward was related to Eliza's grandmother, as they shared the same surname, both living within the same small

[6] Now Helpston, in Cambridgeshire, formerly Helpstone in Northamptonshire.

[7] Pickworth, population in 1851 was 157.

[8] Swinstead, population in 1851 was 490.

community. Then, in 1855, just like her mother, she gave birth to an illegitimate baby at Pickworth on 2 August. The child was a boy and, like Eliza, assumed his mother's surname and was named William Thomas Pridmore. Then, in 1858, Eliza gives birth to another illegitimate son who she named John William, and he, too, assumed the Pridmore name. On the day of the 1861 census (7 April), Eliza is back in Bourn with John William, her widowed grandmother, Elizabeth Pridmore (James Pridmore had passed away in September 1848), and an 11-year-old cousin called Mary Michelson. William Thomas is living with the Fowlers at Pickworth.

On 25 January 1862, Eliza married 27-year-old brick maker William Gilbert at Bourn. Now 6 years old, we might assume that William would have moved to Bourn with his mother and half-brother. We can only speculate, but it would seem that William Thomas was not accepted into the Gilbert family and he continued being brought up by Jane, his maternal grandmother, and Thomas Fowler back in Pickworth. However, John William Pridmore was accepted into the Gilbert family and it is very likely that he was fathered by William Gilbert before he and Eliza married, as John William Pridmore became John William Gilbert. In 1867, John William was presented with a new brother, Thomas Gilbert. Meanwhile, William Thomas Pridmore was still living with Jane and Thomas Fowler.

By 1871, the Gilbert family had moved to 18 Lincoln Lane, Boston, Lincolnshire, where William now worked at the local gas works, and with the addition of another baby son, James Gilbert, born that very year. William Thomas Pridmore, now 15 years old, was still living with his grandparents at Pickworth and working in 'agriculture pursuits', likely as a farm labourer.

On 2 April 1877, William Thomas married 17-year-old Sarah Jane Culpin, who was expecting his child, at the Pickworth Parish Church; Ernest William Pridmore, the first of William and Sarah's thirteen children, was born on 28 July. Sarah Jane was the daughter of Richard and Sarah Ann Culpin (née Crane). Richard Culpin's occupation was recorded on the marriage certificate as a labourer. Two years later, William and Sarah move to Wittering, Northamptonshire, where William continued to work in agriculture as a farm labourer; perhaps work was the reason for their move, as the population of Wittering was in decline and 75% of the male population worked in agriculture,[9]

[9] 1881 Census

thus providing more opportunity for work and possibly higher wages than in Pickworth. On 1 May 1879, Sarah gave birth to their second son, Albert, at Wittering.

In 1880, they moved to Sheffield, where William Thomas was reunited with his mother and the Gilbert family, sharing a house at 138 Sutherland Road, Brightside, where the Gilberts had moved that same year. It is here that a third son, John Thomas, was born on 23 February 1881. John Thomas Pridmore was the first of the family to be born in Sheffield. The two families followed the trend of 19th-century migration from rural to urban life, drawn by the prospects offered by the Industrial Revolution. Despite the smoke and grime and the hard hazardous work of the developing iron and steel industries, not to mention the expanding cutlery trades, in contrast to the relatively less arduous and more peaceful rural existence in Lincolnshire, the potential for higher earnings and better job security offered by the move was enough to entice huge levels of migration. Between 1843 and 1873, the number of people working in the Sheffield cutlery trades trebled and those working in the heavy industries of iron and steel quadrupled. And between 1841 and 1871, the population of Sheffield more than doubled from 111,000 to 240,000.[10]

Late 19th Century Sheffield Post Card Scene by Jotter (author's collection)

---

[10] Drewry, Mick, *Intimidation – The History, The Times and the People of the Sheffield Outrages.* Austin Macauley Publishers, 2017, p. 21.

I can't imagine 138 Sutherland Road being a huge house in what was the heart of Sheffield's industrial east end, so it must have been a tight squeeze for two families of five. At least all of the children were boys and able to share bedrooms. William Gilbert worked in the ironworks with his eldest son, John.

The 1881 census tells us that William Pridmore was an unemployed general labourer, but he got a job at the ironworks by 1883, which is fortunate, as from 1 April, there's another mouth to feed: Arthur Edward, his fourth son, was born on that day.

The addition of another household member would have made a difficult situation even more so, but now that William Pridmore was earning, he was able to move the family to a house of their own, taking residence at 4 Harleston Street in Burngreave in 1884.

On 8 April 1885, Sarah presents him with their first daughter, who they named Florence. Over the next two years, William and Sarah continued their programme of procreation with two more daughters: Beatrice Eliza was born on 6 May 1887 and Lillian May on 12 May 1889.

Sadly, Beatrice died in infancy of pneumonia, about a month before Lillian was born. She was buried at Burngreave Cemetery on 4 April 1889.[11]

The infant mortality rate in Britain during the 19th century was extremely high. Between 1837 and 1842, a little over 50% of deaths registered in Sheffield were children under 5 years old. The death rate for babies under 12 months was 25%; by the 1890s, it was still 20%.[12]

Such statistics were not lost on William and Sarah, as their next child, a boy they called George Richard, born 6 November 1890, died of 'dyspepsia and general wasting' on 29 September the following year. He was buried with Beatrice in Burngreave Cemetery.

During this period, the family moved house, first to 4 Edgar Street,[13] just around the corner from Harleston Street. George Richard died at Court 27, Carlisle Street,[14] despite the census earlier in the year recording the family at Edgar Street. This indicates that they moved to Carlisle Street sometime between the census on 5 April and September.

---

[11] Burngreave Cemetery, Section: C / Grave: 79

[12] Op. cit. Drewry, pp. 25–26

[13] 1891 Census

[14] http://family.nikellom.com/g2/p1195.htm#i29870

Also, in the 1891 census, William is recorded as a stoker of a stationary boiler, a better-paid job than labouring, and Ernest William had started work as an errand lad, probably at the same ironworks as his father.

The 1890s were very productive years for the Pridmore family, and another baby boy was born on 12 March 1892: Wilfred. Then, in the following year, Sarah produced another son on 18 December 1893: Oswald. June 23 1896, saw the arrival of another boy who was named after the baby boy they had lost, naming him George Harry. By this time, the Pridmores had moved house again, this time to Corby Street.

On 16 July 1898, Percy Pridmore was born at Corby Street, and finally, on 6 May 1900, their last issue, Sidney Pridmore, was born at a new residence on Doncaster Street. Meanwhile, tragedy had struck the family once more on 28 July 1899, when Percy, just 12 months old, died of diarrhoea. He, too, was buried at Burngreave Cemetery, but in a separate grave to that of his brother and sister.[15] Thus, the percentage for infant mortality at the time was tragically manifest upon the Pridmore family, with three out of thirteen children—26%—dying in infancy.

Not only were William and Sarah prolific producers of offspring, but they had a rather disorderly existence with regard to finding a place to settle down with their growing family in Sheffield. This may have been down to the continual need to find a bigger house to fit everyone in; we don't know what other factors may have been at play. More moves were to come, but the Pridmore family's constant moving was not out of the ordinary.

In 1901, they moved to 143 Daisy Walk, Netherthorpe; then, in 1909, to 34 Hunt Street, off St Philip's Road, Netherthorpe. The family remained here up to and beyond the Great War years. Both William and Sarah were still living here when they passed away—Sarah Jane on 20 May 1920 and William Thomas on 18 April 1932. They were buried in the same grave at Burngreave Cemetery.[16] Difficult as it is to comprehend, William Thomas outlived ten of his thirteen children.

The quality of all of the houses in which the family lived would have been substandard by modern expectations. All would have been rented from private

[15] Burngreave Cemetery, Section: M2 / Grave: 75

[16] Burngreave Cemetery, Section HH, Grave 5519

landlords (92% of houses in Sheffield were rented at this time[17]), and frequent flitting from one house to another was pretty common. Many of the working-class houses were of the back-to-back build, despite the prohibition on this type being built, enacted in 1864. Fifteen per cent of Sheffield houses—around 16,000—were still of the back-to-back type in 1914, fifty years after their prohibition.[18]

Many houses would also have been situated around a communal court with a shared water standpipe and outdoor toilets, some still of the old privy-midden type that needed emptying by the 'soil man'. Taking a bath would be in a hand-filled tub in front of the one coal fire in the house, or by visiting the slipper baths that had been added to the local swimming pools by this time. Electric lighting was scarce, for it didn't become widespread until the 1920s; gas lighting was still the norm.

By the turn of the century, many of the fledglings had flown the nest. Albert moved out in 1900 to live with Margaret May, who he later married; they went to live together at 19 Burnt Tree Lane, Netherthorpe. On 23 December 1900, Ernest married Elizabeth Ann Waters and moved in with friends Fred and Eliza Hughes at 5 Court 9, Hoyle Street. In 1900, both John and Arthur joined the Army and went to South Africa and Malta, respectively.

On 2 August 1908, Florence married John William Palmer and moved to Hunt Street. Interestingly, William and Sarah moved the family to 34 Hunt Street later that same year, and Florence and John moved into 143 Daisy Walk. Sadly, the propensity for infant mortality was reflected in the next generation, with Ernest and Elizabeth's second child, Eliza, dying of measles nephritis aged 18 months. She too is buried at Burngreave Cemetery.

By the time of the 1911 census, only the four younger children were still at home with William and Sarah at 34 Hunt Street: 19-year-old Wilfred was working as a labourer at a steel foundry; 17-year-old Oswald was a horn buffer; George Harry was a chemist's errand boy; and 10-year-old Sidney was at school. William, at this point, was working as a bricklayer.

It is here that we leave the nuclear Pridmore family and continue the story through the lens of the four subject brothers' lives: John Thomas, Arthur Edward, Albert and George Harry.

---

[17] Lomax, Scott. *The Home Front – Sheffield in the First World War.* Pen & Sword Military, Barnsley, 2014, p. 1.

[18] Ibid., p. 3.

Views of courts off Hollis Croft, Netherthorpe, around 1910

John Thomas Pridmore

We never knew what pain he had,
We never saw him die,
We only know he passed away,
And never said good-bye.[19]

Had John Thomas Pridmore, my great-grandfather, lived to be my age, he would have been around to celebrate my birth. He would have been in my mum and dad's wedding photos and have drunk a toast to the happy couple. Writing this today, over a century after his death, it is hard to imagine that our lives could have touched. As fate determined, he had precious little time with his own children, of whom he had three, let alone his grandchildren and great-grandchildren.

As we know from the previous chapter, John Thomas Pridmore was born on 23 February 1881 and was the first of our Pridmore family to be born in Sheffield. He was probably delivered at home in Sutherland Road, and by a local midwife or 'handywoman',[20] who would charge a few shillings, rather than a general practitioner, who would charge much more. The midwife would also help the mother through the first week or so after the birth, taking care of housework and looking after any other children in the house.

We know nothing of John's early childhood, but he had the company of his siblings growing up and was probably fond of his brothers, especially Ernest

[19] Verse from a memento mori card to John Thomas

[20] Handywoman: a woman with no formal training, but who had learnt what was required through accompanying an experienced midwife through many confinements, and thus was accepted as capable.

William who, being two years his senior, would look out for his little brother. John named his first son, my grandfather, Ernest William. It appears that Ernest had some health issues as an infant and lost a lot of time off school.

By the 1880s, every child between the ages of 5 and 10 had to go to school. The brothers attended All Saints Boys' School on Sutherland Road; girls had their own school in a separate building. Both were attached to the imposing All Saints Church,[21] which could be seen from miles around. Albert started school on 14 February 1887, and John joined him on 11 February 1889, then Arthur on 12 February 1891. The 1891 census tells us that Florence, at 5 years old, had also started school, but she would have been in the infant girls' school next door. Ernest had left school and was now working as an errand boy.

All Saints was a fair-sized school, which opened in 1872, accommodating 1,332 children under head teacher Alfred Edward Kirkham.[22] Victorian schools were very basic and often overcrowded, with up to one hundred pupils per class. Teaching was very much dictatorial, with little opportunity for pupils to ask questions, but simply having to accept what the teacher told them. The emphasis was on the three 'Rs' – reading, writing and arithmetic, with a little history and geography thrown in. Physical education lessons were known as 'drill' and involved running on the spot, marching and stretching, lifting dumbbells, all undertaken in the playground without a change of clothes. Older boys would do woodwork, and girls embroidery and housework. Discipline was harsh, with the indiscriminate use of the cane for both sexes. The maxim was founded on Proverbs 13:24: *'He that spareth his rod hateth his son: but he that loveth him chasteneth him betimes,'* or *'spare the rod and spoil the child.'*

The 1891 census tells us that John was still at school, but he may have left school at 12 or 13, which was the usual age to leave at this time,[23] and found employment of sorts over the next few years, maybe as a labourer for his father, or perhaps on the railways where he would later work. But whatever he did, it would not match his aspiration for adventure that he would seek in 1900 when he applied to join the army. At this time, he was employed as a labourer.

---

[21] All Saints' Church was demolished in June 1977.

[22] Alfred Edward Kirkham was headmaster at All Saints for 40 years. He died on 16 August 1923, aged 71, and is buried at Burngreave Cemetery.

[23] Warr, Peter, *Sheffield in the Great War,* Pen & Sword Military, Barnsley, 2015, p. 46. The school leaving age was fixed at 14 in 1918.

All Saint's Church with the school buildings to the right

Ten days before his 19th birthday, on 13 February 1900, John turned up at the Sheffield army recruiting office to see Sergeant G Henderson for his attestation to be approved, and he was passed fit for the Militia. It is from this record on enlisting that we get a more intimate knowledge of John Thomas Pridmore.

Physically, John was slight by modern standards, but people were much smaller at the turn of the 19th century than they are today. He was just 5 feet 4¼ inches, weighing 117 lbs (8 st 3 lb). He had a 31-inch chest, expanding to 34 inches. He is described as having a fresh complexion, with grey eyes and brown hair. Recorded distinctive marks were a slight brown stain on the right side of his stomach and a slight scar on his face. He declared his religion as the Church of England. The minimum height for the army was 5'3" in 1900; this had been reduced from 5'4" the previous year to allow for more recruits to be sent to the war in South Africa. The age requirement was 18 to 25 years. Whilst John's physique appears to be small, it is worth noting that, at this time, men were on average four inches shorter than they are today.[24]

---

[24] Ibid., p. 45

John swore his oath and signed up for a term of six years as a Militiaman for West Yorkshire in the King's Own Yorkshire Light Infantry (KOYLI) and became Private John Thomas Pridmore 7398 of 3rd Battalion KOYLI. He embarked on his first 49 days of drilling and training and being kitted out at one of the army depots, probably Strensall Common on the outskirts of York or perhaps Pontefract. He successfully completed this initiation, and on 16 June 1900 he joined the regular army and became Private 6640, 2nd Battalion KOYLI. The 3rd Battalion was a territorial battalion and the 2nd Battalion a service battalion.

The war in South Africa—the Boer War—had been raging for nine months when John joined 2/KOYLI. Half of the battalion was one of the first British Army units to arrive there, on 13 October 1899, having hurriedly embarked on HMS *Powerful* from Mauritius, where the battalion had been garrisoned since February 1899. Assuming that he arrived in late June or early July 1900, he would have missed some of the key battles that 2/KOYLI was involved in and to its credit: Belmont, 23 November; Enslin, 25 November; Modder River, 28 November. He also missed 'Black Week', when the British suffered three successive defeats: Stormberg, 10 December; Magersfontein, 11 December; Colenso, 15 December. At Enslin, 2/KOYLI was commended by the official correspondent, who wrote:

'The Royal Navy and the King's Own Yorkshire Light Infantry won the laurels of as hot a fight at Enslin and as plucky a storming of a fortified height as stands to the credit of any Regiment in the Army List. The wiry Yorkshire stock, confident in its continuous experience of war, and hardened by a steady training of months, makes a soldier after the heart of Napoleon; and the silent pride of their motto, Cede nullis, *was more than justified as they swung back into camp as steadily as if the loss of 51 of their best men killed and wounded was no great price to pay for work so well done as theirs.'*[25]

Despite defeat at Magersfontein, 2/KOYLI was still worthy of praise from the Commanding Officer, Lord Methuen, who wrote two days after the battle:

---

[25] Whyte, Wolmer (Ed.), *The Roll of the Drum: Histories of the Regiments of the British Army – The King's Own Yorkshire Light Infantry (K. O. Y. L. I. S.),* Hutchinson & Co (Publishers) Ltd, London, 1940, p. 40.

'The Lieutenant-General fully appreciates the good work done by The King's Own Yorkshire Light Infantry, and he always felt sure that his right was safe with that Regiment in the position it held.'[26]

At Modder River, we find evidence of Sheffield men in *Cassell's History,* where one of the officers leads an attack on a farmhouse holding scores of Boer riflemen strafing the attacking 9th Brigade. After creeping as far as they could under cover, the officer shouts, *'Now, boys!'*

'Then the Tykes tear madly for the building. Here is a door—loopholed, and Mauser muzzles peeping through the holes. Down it goes. Smash! And with the butt-end of their rifles, the Yorkshire Light Infantry smash the thick wood to splinters. "Into them, boys!" "Give them some cold Sheffield!" Boers die on the stairs, and in the kitchen, and in the great parlour where last night they assembled to read the Bible and offer up prayer to the God of battles that he would deliver these Philistines into their hand.'[27]

If John had joined the battalion by 26 June 1900, when a KOYLI piquet was surrounded on three sides by 500 Boers at close quarter at Lindley, he may well have witnessed the action that resulted in the awarding of the Victoria Cross to Private Charles Burley Ward, who volunteered to take a critical message to the signalling station, asking for reinforcements. His request was initially refused, for he was exposing himself as a sure target, but the situation was desperate, and he was allowed to go. Miraculously, he got to the signalling station untouched by the bullets flying around him and was able to deliver the message. He could have remained behind the line, but he returned to his comrades to let his commanding officer know that reinforcements had been requested. This time, he wasn't so lucky and caught a bullet in his arm, and was severely wounded. The official account in his medal citation states: *'but for his gallant action, the post would certainly have been captured.'*

Charles Ward had the privilege of being the last VC recipient to be divested by Queen Victoria: he was the lowest rank and last in line of the five recipients

---

[26] Ibid., p. 41

[27] Cassell's *History of the Boer War, 1899–1902, vol. I* (London: Cassell and Company, 1903), p. 262.

presented with the VC by the Queen at Windsor Castle in December 1900; she died a few weeks later.[28]

Two officers were wounded, and six of the men were killed or wounded during this exchange with the Boers. Was John one of the survivors? Of course, we will never know; we can't even be sure that he had arrived in South Africa at this point, but the action at Lindley was typical of the encounters he was about to endure. What we can do is follow the 2/KOYLI on its campaign from around the time that John may have joined it.

Private Charles Burley Ward VC

The Second Boer War was a new type of warfare, and something the British Army had to quickly adapt to. Prior to the Boer War, and since Waterloo, with the exception of the Crimean War, which never threatened Britain or its colonies, the British Army had not fought a major war, only encounters with the 'natives' of the British colonies when rebellions and uprisings occurred against the expansion of Empire, the largest of which was the Indian Rebellion of 1857. The

---

[28] westernfrontassociation.com/world-war-i-articles/queen-victoria-s-last-vc/

First Boer War, from December 1880 to 23 March 1881, was such a rebellion against Britain's annexation of the Transvaal in 1877. Britain now faced organised armies with the latest Mauser rifles and modern artillery—what was, in essence, a preamble to what would come in 1914.

In addition to facing a relatively well-armed, modern enemy, the British Army had to contend with the South African environment and its unpredictable weather, something the Boers were used to and would use to their advantage. The British soldiers weren't used to the flies and the dust; the heat of the midday sun and the cold of the nights; the sudden storms. Then there was the lack of clean water, and a diet of army biscuits and bully beef. They were also susceptible to disease, in particular, enteric fever, for which there was no cure. Of the 27,000 British soldiers who died in the Boer War, 13,250 died from disease. Another 31,000 were invalided home because of it, and some of them would also succumb.[29] If John thought he was in for adventure, I'm pretty sure it wasn't what he had hoped for.

By October 1900, the war had developed into a guerrilla war. There would be no more set battles, but dozens of small skirmishes that would last for the next eighteen months. The British Army would suffer more casualties in those eighteen months than it had in all the previous battles.[30]

On Monday, 3 December 1900, twenty-one men of 2/KOYLI were engaged in one of these skirmishes near Rustenberg. A large convoy of wagons, stretching 3 km along the Pretoria-Rustenberg road, was attacked by 600 Boers, who successfully looted 26 of the fully loaded wagons. British casualties were 18 killed and 22 wounded. These included 5 killed and 6 severely wounded KOYLIs. Amongst the wounded was the leader of the detachment, Lance-Corporal G Miller, who was awarded the Distinguished Conduct Medal (DCM).

The likelihood of John being involved in this action is minimal, but he could have been; we will never know.

---

[29] Farwell, Bryon, *The Great Boer War*, Wordsworth Military Library, Wordsworth Edition, Ware, Hertfordshire, 1999, p. 241.

[30] Ibid., p. 324.

KOYLI Sergeant 1898

On 13 December, just ten days after the action near Rustenberg, the 2/KOYLI was involved in a larger encounter at the British camp of around 1,500 men at Nooitgedacht.[31] A commando[32] of 600 Boers, led by Koos de la Rey, one of the major Boer leaders, had been scouting the camp for several days when it was joined by a second commando of 1,500 men. This gave them numerical superiority over the British, who were positioned in what was a vulnerable position for a base. The Boers' raid resulted in the loss of half of the British brigade and much of its supplies. Four companies of 2/KOYLI covered the retirement of what remained of the brigade, along with its artillery, towards Pretoria. Again, John could have been involved in this engagement.

---

[31] Op. cit. Whyte, p. 42.

[32] Commando: a military unit of the Boers, trained and organised as shock troops, especially for hit-and-run raids into enemy territory.

By October 1901, 2/KOYLI was garrisoned at Elandsfontein, and on 31 October, they marched to assist Lieutenant-Colonel G.E. Benson's column of Royal Artillery at Bakenlaagte in the Eastern Transvaal, where it had been attacked and smashed by a numerically superior Boer contingent. Over a quarter of his men were killed and over a third wounded; Benson was among the casualties, killed by a sniper's bullet.[33]I have found little mention of 2/KOYLI in the histories that I have used since the actions above and up until the end of the War, when it was recorded as being in blockhouses[34] around Ermelo. The British Army faced many skirmishes with Boer commandos during this phase of the war, and 2/KOYLI would have been involved in some of them, with John amongst the combatants.

It was during this period that the British adopted a scorched earth policy towards civilians helping the Boer commandos. Farmsteads were torched, livestock slaughtered, crops destroyed, and many people, mostly women and children, were left with little choice but to turn to British 'protection' in 'refuge camps'. When we think of concentration camps, we immediately think of the Nazis, but it was the British who were the first to establish them during the Boer War. And as with the Nazi's camps, many people died in the British camps, again, mainly children:

'More Boer boys and girls under the age of sixteen died in British concentration camps than all the fighting men killed by bullets and shells on both sides in the course of the entire war.'[35]

Estimates of the numbers of Boers and African civilians dying in the concentration camps vary, with one suggesting that 22,000 children died in the camps, the majority from epidemics of measles and typhoid, which could have been avoided. It is hard to contemplate that John might have been posted to guard one of these abominable places, but it is a possibility. Rather, I imagine him manning one of the blockhouses.

---

[33] angloboerwar.com/forum

[34] Blockhouses were lines of tin and concrete structures, within rifle range of each other, linked with barbed wire fences, towards which Boer columns were to be driven and snared.

Pakenham, Thomas, *The Boer War*, Weidenfeld and Nicolson, London, 1979, p. 499.

[35] Op. cit. Farwell, p. 392.

Wherever he was, and whatever actions he was involved in during his time in South Africa, there is little doubt that the Boer War was a real eye-opener for John. Whatever sense of adventure he may have had would have been shattered by the reality of his experience. The reality of war – modern war – would have been darker than he imagined. The casualties were not mere statistics but real people, people with whom he lived and fought, men with whom he had shared the adventure until the fatal blow.

And that fatal blow wouldn't always be clean. A bullet and instant death was the cleanest way to go, but many of his comrades would have died from artillery shells and shrapnel, leaving an ugly, mangled mess of flesh, bone and blood; so much so that they had to be buried there and then, without ceremony. Many others would have succumbed to their wounds or to disease in the shamefully inadequate army hospitals.

Whilst surviving physically – we don't know if he was wounded at all – one can only begin to imagine the mental scars that this would have left on John.

Example of a Blockhouse, East Transvaal (author's collection)

However, John fared well during the War. By the end of his time in South Africa, he had been promoted to Lance Corporal, which suggests he had impressed his commanders and served his Queen and country well. We know of his promotion from the Queen's South Africa Medal Roll of Honours.[36]

[36] National Archives, WO 100/194

On Saturday, 31 May 1902, the Boer leaders finally surrendered and hostilities came to an end. The 2/KOYLI remained in South Africa until October, no doubt helping with the military administration of the Peace Treaty of Vereeniging.[37] The battalion embarked at Durban on the *S.S. Staffordshire* on 7 October 1902 and disembarked at Malta on 28 October, where they would make base at St George's Barracks, Pembroke. In the following year, three companies and the HQ Company embarked on the *M.S. Dunera* for Crete; 500 men remained in Malta. John was in one of the companies bound for Crete. Whilst in Crete, he posed for a studio photo to send back home.

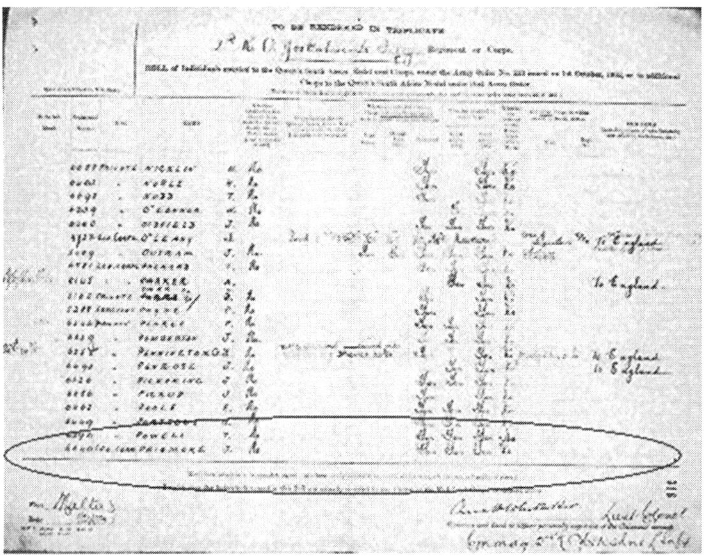

Queens South Africa Medal Roll of Honours (National Archives)

On 1 February 1903, whilst in Malta, John was presented with his Queen's South Africa Medal at Gozo Barracks. On 1 March 1905, the 2/KOYLI embarked for England, where it spent time in Sheffield and Strensall, York. It was in Sheffield, in July 1905, that the battalion was presented with new colours by King Edward VII. Whilst at Strensall, John met Harriet Annie Myton, and on leaving the army when his six years were up in 1906, he stayed with her in York.

[37] The Peace Treaty of Vereeniging was negotiated by the British and the Boer leaders acting on behalf of the Government of South African Republic to end hostilities and to agree the ten articles of settlement.

Harriet Annie Myton was born on 6 September 1886 at 8 St Saviour's Court, St Saviour, York. Her mother was Annie Myton, a domestic servant, but no father is recorded on the birth certificate. As with John's father and grandmother, Harriet adopted her mother's surname. On the 1891 census form, she is listed as living at 69 Stainford Street, St Mary's, and attending Bishophill Junior School, residing with her grandparents, James and Charlotte Myton. Also in the household is her 15-year-old brother, Walter, but her mother isn't present. By 1901, aged 14, Harriet is a live-in domestic servant at 10 St Oswald's Road, working for Charles and Elizabeth Atkinson. John and Harriet were married on 15 February 1907 at the York registry office; she is recorded as a 21-year-old servant. They moved into 18 Swinegate, in the centre of York.[38]

John Thomas Pridmore in Crete 1904 or 1905 (author's collection)

[38] 18 Swinegate is now a barbers' shop, and the area was the subject of an archaeological excavation in 1990.

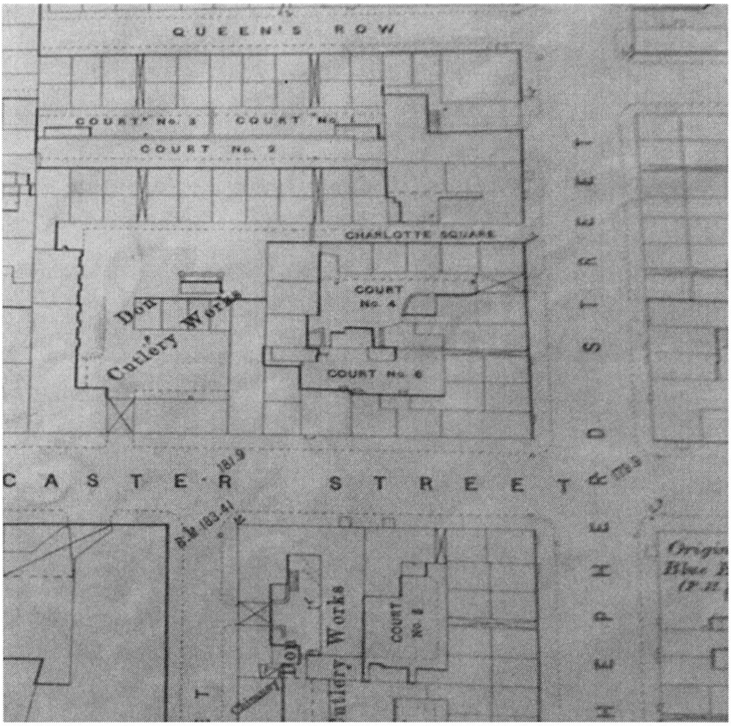

4 Court, Shepherd Street

On 13 March 1908, and still living at 18 Swinegate, Harriet presented John with their first child, Ernest William, my grandfather. During 1910, John and a pregnant Harriet move to Sheffield with young Ernest William to live with John's eldest brother, Ernest, at 4 Court, 6 House, Shepherd Street, where Ernest and his family had lived since 1901. John got a job labouring on the railways. On 3 May 1910, Harriet gave birth to their second child, a daughter who they named Gladys. By the time of the 1911 census, John had moved his family to a home of their own at 4 Court, Number 1 House, Hunt Street, and was now a railway porter. On 14 July 1913, their third and final child, Frederick, was born at Hunt Street. John was now working in the steelworks as a labourer.

Number 1 House at 4 Court, Hunt Street, consisted of only three rooms. The construction would have been similar to the back-to-back cottage that I lived in as a young boy at 7 Court, Number 1 House, Bradfield Road, in Owlerton. There were three storeys, each of one room, with the top room having an open stairwell. The room on the ground floor was both a living room and a kitchen, with a pot sink in one corner. There was a fireplace in the centre that once housed a Yorkshire range; by the 1950s, this had been removed and replaced with a tiled fire surround and open coal fire. Cooking was now done on a gas cooker at the side of the sink. A small cellar/pantry took up a portion of the house footprint, which made this room the smallest in the house. The bedroom on the second floor was slightly bigger, with the landing and staircase over the pantry. The third-floor attic bedroom had more space due to the open stairwell.

This very house was the subject of a Police Court case in 1917, when it was found that three families, consisting of 14 to 15 individuals, mostly children, were living there in filthy conditions.[39] To my horror, I found that these families, all related, were my ancestors, one individual was my paternal grandmother. It appears that this house had been occupied by at least three generations of my paternal family.[40] It is ironic that, whilst researching one side of my family, I uncovered a shameful episode in the history of the other. And yet, there is a connection with the Pridmores, as one of the children involved, my step-aunt, later married my maternal grandfather, the now widower Ernest William, the eldest son of John Thomas.

Examples of such three-roomed houses still exist in Sheffield, but I doubt that any are still inhabited; they are now used for industrial storage or simply not used at all, such as those I photographed for my *Sheffield Outrages* book in 2017.[41]

As John was settling down to family life, war clouds were looming once more, this time over Europe, where the King's cousin, the German Kaiser Wilhelm II, was building his army and navy with an expansionist vision; where France was looking to avenge its defeat in the Franco-Prussian War of 1870–1871; and where Britain was attempting to isolate the now united Germany.

The history of the Great War is well documented, and I am no military historian – although I have read much military history over the years, and I have had to read more to inform the writing of this book – so I will limit the narrative to the events that the Pridmore brothers were probably involved in up until their deaths, and any other information that is relevant to the story.

---

[39] Op. cit. Lomax, p. 192

[40] *Yorkshire Telegraph and Star,* 23 August 1917 and *Sheffield Daily Telegraph,* 24 August 1917

[41] Op. cit. Drewry, p. 30

For Britain, the Great War officially began at 11.00pm on Monday, 4 August 1914, as the deadline for Britain's ultimatum to Germany expired following its invasion of Belgium in the early hours of that day. Like most of Britain, the people of Sheffield had anxiously waited for a decision to be made by the government following the news of Germany's aggression and Britain's ultimatum. That news came direct from King George V a short time after the ultimatum had expired, stating that Britain was now at war with Germany.

Sheffield was quick to respond to the call for men to join the armed forces, and during August and September 1914, 10,719 of its eligible recruits enlisted.[42] Most of those who joined the Army enlisted into either the York & Lancaster Regiment or the King's Own Yorkshire Light Infantry, with the York & Lancs forming the 4th (Hallamshire) Territorial Battalion[43]. In its duration, a total of 52,000 Sheffield men left to fight in the Great War; around 6,000 of these died.[44]

Most of the new recruits joined a New Army battalion, also known as a Kitchener's Army battalion, after the Secretary of State for War, Herbert Kitchener, and didn't expect to see service at the Front until mid-1916, but circumstances dictated an earlier introduction to the action. The inexperienced would need to be trained by regular NCOs and veteran officers brought back from retirement for their experience, such as Lieutenant-Colonel Percy Holland, a retired Indian Army officer who was given command of the new KOYLI recruits in Sheffield.

One young Sheffield lad, Lancelot Spicer, found his introduction to Army life very basic:

'All the men were in civilian clothes, and all we had for training were wooden rifles. Apart from the officers, the only ones in uniform were a few non-commissioned officers who were regulars. The Commanding Officer was Lt Col Holland, a retired Indian Army officer ... a pleasant enough old boy, but his soldiering appeared to us young raw recruits to be of the Indian Mutiny – in battalion parades he would ask in a loud voice "Mr Butler (the adjutant), how many white officers on parade?"'[45]

---

[42] Op. cit. Lomax, p. 35

[43] Ibid., p. 21

[44] Op. cit. Warr, p. 19

[45] Holmes, Richard, *Tommy – The British Soldier on the Western Front 1914–1918,* Harper Collins Publishers, London, 2004, p. 83

The British Army at this time had been recruited mainly from the cities and the bigger towns, with the greater number of men being unskilled labourers, many of them joining from the ranks of the unemployed. A report of 1909 disclosed that 90% of those applying to enrol and undertaking medical examination for their fitness were out of work; for them, the Army was the only option for earning a living, and driven by what a senior Army officer at the time called *'compulsion of destitution'*.[46]

The British Expeditionary Force that went to France in 1914 was still very much a Victorian army, steeped in its colonial history, the myths of the 19th century and, of course, its recent experiences in South Africa. Britain's standing army consisted of just over 250,000 Regulars. Added to this were 250,000 Territorial and 200,000 Reservists, totalling around 700,000 trained soldiers.[47]

At the outbreak of the War, there were five KOYLI battalions. 1/KOYLI was in Singapore, where it remained until September, arriving back in England on 9 November. 3/KOYLI was undergoing training at Strensall Camp and was moved to Pontefract when notice to mobilise was received. 4 and 5/KOYLI were undertaking annual training at Whitby. 2/KOYLI was in Ireland, having spent 10 months at Portobello Barracks in Dublin, which was in a state of civil unrest.

2/KOYLI was under strength; it was short of 7 officers, 19 sergeants and 596 rank and file to complete establishment for war service.[48] Reservists were sent from Pontefract to make up the shortfall of the battalion. These were made up of officers from the War Office, currently on staff duties or on training at the Staff College, and others transferred from other regiments: Captain R.S. Ledger from 1/Green Howards, and Lieutenant J.B.L. Noel and 2nd Lieutenant H.J. Hardiman from 2/East Yorkshire Regiment[49]. The complement of a battalion in the British Army of 1914 was 35 officers and 1,000 other ranks.[50] Back in Pontefract, a new service battalion was being mobilised that would become 6/KOYLI.

---

[46] Beckett, Ian F.W., *Ypres The First Battle 1914*, Routledge, London, 2013, p. 37–38.

[47] National Army Museum website: 1914: To arms, nam.ac.uk/explore/to-arms1914

[48] Bond, R.C., *The King's Own Yorkshire Light Infantry in the Great War – Volume III*, Percy Lund, Humphries & Co Ltd, Bradford, 1929, p. 714.

[49] Ibid., p. 715.

[50] The regular battalion of the British Army consisted of four companies, each of 5 officers and 240 men. A brigade consisted of four battalions: approximately 140 officers and 4,000 men.

John would not have been involved in the mobilisation of 2/KOYLI, as he did not re-enlist until the War was declared, and it would have taken some time for him to undertake the necessary checks, administration requirements and perhaps some induction training. His medals and clasp record shows that he joined the 2nd Battalion on 11 September 1914. He didn't receive the rank of Lance-Corporal that he had won in South Africa, and joined the ranks of Privates of his old regiment and battalion.

However, Arthur, who had remained in the Army, was one of the first of the British Expeditionary Force to land in France, his medals and clasp qualifying date being 10 August 1914, and he would have been part of the story so far. I shall return to this juncture in the next chapter.

Arthur Edward Pridmore

Who made the law that men should die in meadows?
Who spake the word that blood should splash the lanes?
Who gave it forth that gardens should be boneyards?
Who spread the hills with flesh, and blood, and brains?[51]

As told in Chapter 1, Arthur Edward Pridmore, William and Sarah's fourth child and fourth son, was born on 1 April 1883 at the overcrowded 138 Sutherland Road. His grandmother, Eliza, registered the birth. As also indicated in the first chapter, the Pridmore family moved to their own house the following year, at 4 Harleston Street. Now established in a Sheffield home of their own, the family continued to grow, and Arthur was blessed with siblings to watch out for, and for them to watch out for him, as he grew up in the shadows of towering chimneys and the smoke clouds that they belched out over the huge steel works of the East End. Unlike his eldest brother, Ernest, he would seem to have got through childhood without suffering any major health problems. And unlike three of his siblings, he actually survived childhood, and by 1901 Arthur is employed as a labourer in a local brewery and now living with his parents and his younger brothers and sisters at 143 Daisy Walk; Ernest and Albert having moved out to begin their own families, and John now in the Army, undertaking his training before embarking for South Africa.

Arthur enlisted soon after his 18th birthday and, like John, joined 3rd Battalion King's Own Yorkshire Light Infantry. Whilst John went on to join the Regular Army with 2/KOYLI, Arthur remained in 3/KOYLI, a territorial

[51] Leslie Coulson, war poet and sergeant, 12/ London, killed at Leuze Wood, 7 October 1916.

battalion. Whilst territorial battalions were designated non-combatant and were not to serve overseas, 3/KOYLI was sent to Malta and arrived there in June 1901. It is likely that, once he had finished his induction training at Pontefract, Private 7646 Arthur Edward Pridmore was amongst the Yorkshire men disembarking at Malta and destined to be based at the Gozo Garrison, where he was to receive his Mediterranean Medal on 1 February 1902. According to one source, Arthur also served in Gibraltar, but I have been unable to verify this.

On 23 March 1902, 3/KOYLI embarked for Liverpool on the Screw Steamer *Menes*. The 3/KOYLI complement on the passenger list included the HQ Company and 6 Companies: 10 officers, 1 officer's wife and 3 children, 1 Warrant Officer, 29 Sergeants, 3 Buglers, 425 rank & file, 4 soldiers' wives and 11 children. The men disembarked on 2 April 1902.[52]

In 1908, following the Territorial and Reserve Forces Act of 1907, 3/KOYLI was transferred to the Special Reserves, the new name for the Militia, and based at Pontefract. It is possible that by this time, Arthur had already transferred to 2/KOYLI, and his service number had changed to 7171; according to service number records, numbers 7436–8107 correspond to those issued between 23 June 1903 and 25 January 1904.

In November 1907, 2/KOYLI left Sheffield and moved to Aldershot. It is here that Arthur met Annie Ashworth, a widow whose late husband was probably one of a number of Boer War casualties of that name. Annie was from a military family. Born Annie Langley at the Curragh[53] in Ireland, she was the daughter of the late Sergeant Major Samuel Langley of 1st Battalion King's Dragoon Guards. Arthur and Annie married at St Michael's Parish Church, Aldershot, on 8 March 1909; Annie was 29 years old.

At the time of the census two years later (2 April 1911), Arthur and Annie were living back in Yorkshire at 41 Halifax Road, Dewsbury. They didn't have children of their own, but also on the 1911 census form was a visitor to the household, one 5-weeks-old Leslie Frederick John Dyer. Despite searching for information about Leslie Dyer, what connection he had with Arthur and Annie remains a mystery. The only thing that I found was that Leslie Frederick John Dyer died in the third quarter of 1937, aged 26, in Surrey; this must be the same man, and his relationship to the Pridmores remains a mystery.

---

[52] *https://www.angloboerwar.com/boer-war*

[53] The Curragh has been the site of a military camp since 1856, and remains the home of the Defence Forces Training Centre of the Irish Defence Forces.

By 1911, Arthur was a recruiting sergeant, which throws up an anomaly, as recruiting sergeants were not regulars but territorial, suggesting that he was still in 3/KOYLI in 1911. On the outbreak of war in August 1914, 3/KOYLI moved to Hull to help defend against any possible invasion. It could be that it was then that Arthur moved to 2/KOYLI, as many reservists were called up for the regular army.

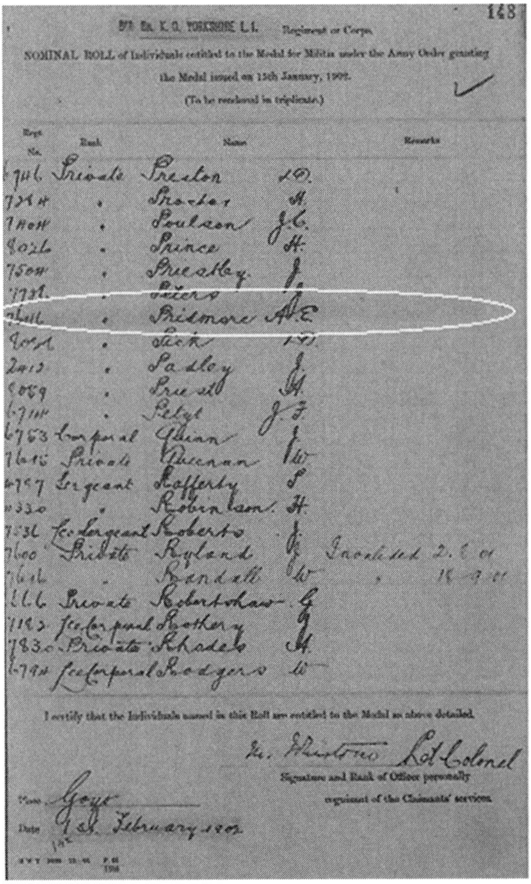
Regiment or Corps.

NOMINAL ROLL of Individuals entitled to the Medal for Militia under the Army Order granting the Medal issued on 15th January, 1903.

(To be rendered in triplicate.)

Regt. No.	Rank	Name	Remarks

I certify that the Individuals named in this Roll are entitled to the Medal as above detailed.

Signature and Rank of Officer personally cognisant of the Claimants' services.

Place

Date

Mediterranean Medal for Militia Roll[54]

2/KOYLI embarked on the *S.S. Buteshire* at the North Wall, Dublin, at 5.00pm on 14 August, and the ship got under way at 7.00pm.[55] There were three disembarkation ports in France: Le Havre, with a capacity to receive 30 ships per

[54] The Public Record Office, Reference WO 100/368.

[55] Ibid., p. 716.

day; Rouen, 20 ships per day; and Boulogne, 11 ships per day.[56] Their destination was not known until the *Buteshire* arrived at Le Havre on Sunday, 16 August, and disembarkation commenced at 11.00pm.

The men slept in a huge shed on the quayside, and on the following day at 6.30pm, the Battalion left for the front on one of the 25 trains per day that departed from Le Havre Railway Station, finally arriving at Landrecies at midday on 18 August after a slow journey through Rouen, Amiens and Busigny, stopping at checkpoints along the way at bridges and culverts manned by the French police.[57] That evening, the Battalion joined the 13th Infantry Brigade at Maroilles.[58]

The 13th Infantry Brigade consisted of 2/KOYLI, 2/King's Own Scottish Borderers (KOSB), 2/Duke of Wellington's (West Riding) Regiment, and 1/Queen's Own (Royal West Kent) Regiment, under the command of Brigadier-General G.J. Cuthbert, C.B.[59]

On 20 August, each of the battalions was ominously addressed by the General Officer Commanding (GOC) 5th Division, Major General Sir Charles Fergusson:

'There must be no surrender, men must fight to the last, with their fists if their rifles are useless; this will be a war of self-sacrifice; possibly whole battalions, even brigades, may have to be sacrificed in order to make it good for others.'[60]

The 21 August was spent on the march to the front, through Bavai to the outpost line between Houdain and Taisnieres. On the morning of Saturday, 22 August, the 13th Brigade crossed the Belgian frontier and marched on to Boussu,

---

[56] Neillands, Robin, *The Old Contemptibles – The British Expeditionary Force, 1914.* John Murray, London, 2004, p. 91.

[57] Op. cit. Bond, p. 716–717.

[58] Ibid.

[59] Edmonds, Brigadier-General J.E. *Official History of the Great War – Military Operations France & Belgium 1914, Vol. I.* The Naval & Military Press Ltd and The Imperial War Museum, London, p. 478.

[60] Op. cit. Bond, p. 717.

where the men were welcomed by the locals and took up accommodation in the buildings of a local brewery near to the railway station.[61]

Order of Command at the Battle of Le Cateau, 26 August 1914

II Corps

Sir Horace Smith-Dorrien

↓

5th Division

General Officer Commanding—Major General Sir C. Fergusson

↓

13th Brigade

Brigadier General G. Cuthbert

↓

Battalions:

2/King's Own Scottish Borderers (Lieutenant Colonel C.N. Stephenson)
2/Duke of Wellington's Regiment (Lieutenant Colonel J.A.C. Gibbs)
1/Queen's Royal West Kent (Lieutenant Colonel A. Martyn)
2/King's Own Yorkshire Light Infantry (Lieutenant Colonel R. Bond)

The heavily outnumbered British Expeditionary Force (BEF) was in retreat from Mons, and the 13th Brigade was ordered to hold the line along the Mons-Condé Canal between Les Herbieres and Mariette, with two battalions on outpost duty along a 3-mile front; 2/KOYLI was in support. However, the KOYLI Machine Gun Detachment, led by 2nd Lieutenant John Pepys,[62] was positioned in the front line supporting the defence of the bridge over the canal.

---

[61] Op. cit. Whyte, p. 46.

[62] 2nd Lieutenant John Pepys, aged 24, was the eldest son of Captain Arthur Pepys, 60th Rifles (King's Royal Rifle Corps), of Knowle House, Budleigh Salterton, Devon. Born at Budleigh Salterton, 7 May 1890. Educated at Charterhouse and the Royal Military College, Sandhurst. Gazetted 2nd Lieutenant, 2/KOYLI, 9 November 1910. Buried at Haurage Military Cemetery, Grave number 2A6. His younger brother, 2nd Lieutenant Francis Pepys, Oxfordshire & Buckinghamshire Light Infantry, was killed in action at Ypres, 12 November 1914. Op. cit. De Ruvigny, Vol. 1, p. 287.

John Pepys.

On the following day, Sunday 23 August, the men of 2/KOYLI had their dinner interrupted by German shells falling around the brewery, and they sustained their first casualty: 2nd Lieutenant John Pepys, killed by a sniper's bullet. They quickly finished eating and took up position in support of 2/KOSB, which was sustaining many casualties, so much so that the KOSB's position was taken over by 2/KOYLI sometime between 6.00–7.00pm. At 10.00pm, the battalion was ordered to withdraw to a pre-arranged position by Wasmes, resting for two and a half hours in a cornfield on the way and arriving just before dawn. The men of the Machine Gun Detachment were the last to withdraw, taking with them the body of Lt Pepys. 2nd Lt Pepys was buried by his detachment on the outskirts of Wasmes at dawn the following day.[63]

By 6.00am, the battalion was holding a position in the new front line with 'A' and 'B' Companies, the rest in support. However, as the Germans prepared to attack, they received orders to withdraw and to take up an extended position to cover the approach to the Bavai Road. This was soon followed by orders to renew the withdrawal of the 13th Brigade. That night, as the brigade bivouacked in a field one and a half miles from Bavai, a roll call of 2/KOYLI found one officer (2nd Lt Pepys) had been killed, and 27 other ranks were missing.

---

[63] Op. cit. Bond, p. 720.

At 3.15am on the morning of Monday, 25 August, the battalion continued the retreat towards Le Cateau, reaching their destination in the middle of the afternoon after a gruelling march under a blazing sun. At 2.35pm, the order for a further retirement arrived, but this time, 2/KOSB and 2/KOYLI were to form the rearguard. The following day, just ten days after disembarking in France, would see the 2/KOYLI's first notable battle of the Great War: the Battle of Le Cateau.[64]

*****

The Battle of Le Cateau

The Battle of Le Cateau is well documented, with numerous books having been written specifically covering the action in detail. This I do not intend doing, as not only could I do it justice, but it would overwhelm the narrative of the Pridmore brothers' story at this juncture. John and Arthur entered the war as members of 2/KOYLI, albeit a month apart. John arrived in France two weeks after the Battle of Le Cateau, but Arthur would have been in the thick of it and would have participated in the prelude of the battle, which involved 2/KOYLI. It is with this in mind that I shall only cover the action of 2/KOYLI, one of 40 battalions at Le Cateau, and, where relevant, other battalions of the 13th Brigade. Of course, we have no means of determining exactly where Arthur was at any given time—we don't even know which company of the battalion he was a member of—but we can certainly imagine what he would have been going through. We will also meet other members of 2/KOYLI whose bravery has been noted and rewarded; like John and Arthur, they were all 'brothers in arms'.

Arthur arrived in France on 10 August 1914, which means he was there before 2/KOYLI arrived from Ireland. He probably spent time at the 13th Infantry Brigade base camp at Maroilles until the battalion arrived there on the eighteenth. On 23 August, he and the rest of the battalion got their first taste of war from the German Artillery welcoming them to the Great War. Arthur was the first of the Pridmore brothers to be involved in the action.

The original intention was for the Cavalry Division to take up the rearguard as the retreat from Mons was renewed, but the orders were received late in the

---

64 Op. cit. Whyte, p. 46.

evening of 25 August, and the cavalry brigades were too scattered and exhausted to satisfactorily undertake the role. General Smith-Dorrien, II Corps Commander, decided he would have to make a stand. 2/KOSB Companies took up a position to the left of three 2/KOYLI Companies facing the Cambrai Road, and the other 2/KOSB companies protected their flank on the left. 'A', 'C' and 'D' Companies of 2/KOYLI faced the road in shallow trenches,[65] and 'B' Company took up a position on the right flank by the Reumont–Bavai Road along with the KOYLI Machine Gun Detachment. Two other 2/KOSB Companies were positioned to support their comrades on the front and on the left flank.

To complicate matters, a number of batteries of the Royal Field Artillery (RFA), normally positioned well behind the infantry, were positioned in the front line. This left the batteries exposed and difficult to extract once the withdrawal was resumed. They also attracted German gunfire, which the infantry would also have to endure.

At around 5.00am, the battle began with a German Artillery bombardment of the 13th Brigade positions, simultaneous to an attack by the German Infantry on the British battalions retreating through the town of Le Cateau to their right. At 6.00am, Lieutenant-Colonel Bond, Officer Commanding 2/KOYLI, received an order from Brigadier-General Cuthbert:

'Orders have been changed. There will now be NO retirement for fighting troops. Fill up your trenches with water, food and ammunition, as far as you can.'[66]

Clearly, this was to be a fight to the bitter end and, for many, a requirement for self-sacrifice. The order was confirmed by Staff Officer Colonel Romer, who rode over from II Corps HQ to KOYLI HQ and repeated the order of 'no retirement.'

The German bombardment continued, destroying telephone wires, which made communication between the Companies and HQ impossible, except by runner. High-explosive and shrapnel shells burst all around the RFA batteries. Enemy machine gunners established a position in the crest of a cutting by the

---

[65] These trenches were no more than hastily-dug rifle pits and bore no resemblance to the labyrinth of deep trenches that became the embodiment of the War later on.

[66] Op. cit. Bond, p. 724.

Cambrai road, and men from 2/KOYLI were caught up in their fire, along with rifle fire from the advancing German Infantry. The men could see the ebb and flow of the action between the Germans and the Suffolk Regiment to their right, over the Bavai road towards the town of Le Cateau, which had been taken by the Germans in the early hours of the morning. When the Germans advanced, 2/KOYLI's right flank was exposed.

By around 11.00am, the Germans had advanced to within range of 'B' Company, positioned on the Reumont road. As they approached within 600 yards, the rifles of 'B' Company fired their first rounds, and from this moment, they were constantly engaged in the battle.

British Infantry marching through a French village on the way to Le Cateau (britishbattles.com/first-world-war/battle-of-le-cateau/)

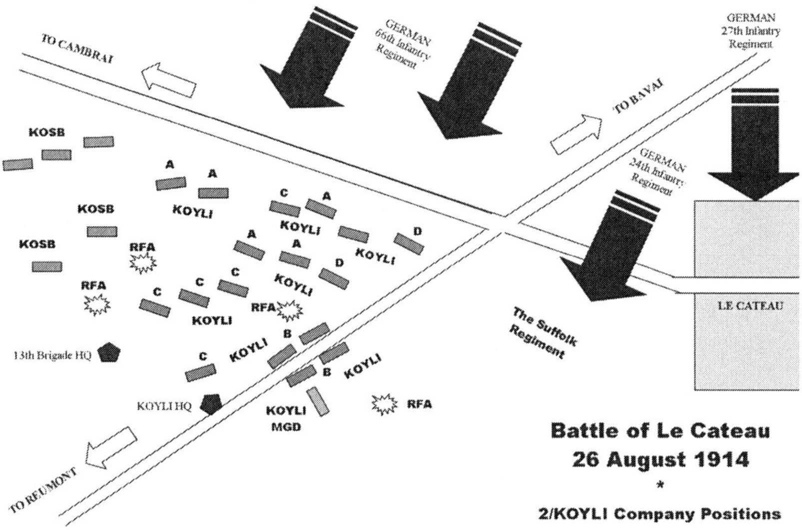

By now, all four 2/KOYLI Companies were in action repelling the attacking German Infantry: 'A', 'C' and 'D' Companies along the front, and 'B' Company and the KOYLI Machine Gun Detachment on the right flank. There is little doubt that Arthur was involved in the action, whichever company he was assigned to, and being a Sergeant, he would have had responsibility for a section of that company; typically, a Sergeant took charge of a platoon of around 30 men.

The German Infantry took heavy losses in their frontal attack, having to cross open land towards the 2/KOYLI trenches, making them easy targets for the Yorkshire and Scottish marksmen. But the attack was relentless, and the Germans managed to establish a position above the KOSB trenches, from where they were able to enfilade the KOYLI Companies. 'A' Company, on the left of the line, fought tenaciously to prevent a German machine gun detachment from taking up an advantageous position, but eventually failed, exposing the KOYLI line to its deadly rapid fire.

The German bombardment of the RFA batteries supporting 2/KOYLI continued until shortly after midday to devastating effect, and at 12.45pm an order was given to extract any of the guns in the centre that could be moved to the rear; just two guns were removed.[67] Evidence of the impact of the German bombardment of the RFA was manifest in the silence of the remaining four guns, and the bodies of their crews and horses lying all around them.

---

[67] Ibid., p. 726.

Lieutenant-Colonel Bond describes the RFA's action at Le Cateau as *'a day of self-sacrifice; as long as there were men left and guns to fire, some reply was made.'*[68]

Bodies of men and horses around abandoned 18-Pounder British field guns at Le Cateau[69]

There followed a lull in the German bombardment for around thirty minutes, but the rattle of rifle fire and the rapid clatter of the machine guns continued up and down the line. When the German bombardment recommenced, it was directed at the infantry trenches, causing many casualties among the KOYLI Companies on the front line. So bad were the casualties that reinforcements were needed at the front to hold the line. At 1.30pm, 'C' Company positions behind the front sent more men forward to make up for the losses.

Two hours later, the trenches were being so badly affected by concentrated German machine-gun fire that they attempted to retire to their original position. Once more, this meant a dash across open land, with the consequential exposure

[68] Ibid.

[69] *https://www.britishbattles.com/first-world-war/battle-of-le-cateau/*

and inevitable losses, which included Lieutenant T.B. Butt, who was wounded, and Sergeant Alfred Walter Patterson, being killed.[70]

'B' Company, on the right flank, continued its action against two battalions of the German 24th Infantry Regiment, which was getting the better of the Suffolks. But by around 2.30pm, two of the KOYLI Machine Gun Detachment's guns had been knocked out. Sergeant Nunn of the MGD had been wounded, along with several of his men. Lieutenant Unett, their CO, ordered the remaining gun to be taken to the nearest 'B' Company trench, where it was broken up. He then retired to KOYLI HQ. Meanwhile, 'B' Company drove back the advance of the German battalions on the right flank, having suffered heavy losses.

'D' Company also suffered heavy casualties, and 'A' Company was running out of ammunition. At 3.25pm, two 'C' Company platoons made a dash across the intervening open land to reinforce the 'A' Company trenches and were met by a devastating storm of bullets. Just 12 men made it to the relative safety of the trenches.[71] The front-line trenches maintained their stand against overwhelming odds, by now surrounded on three sides, until the order to retire eventually came at around 3.30pm. In the last hour, 2/KOYLI stood seemingly alone in stemming the German Infantry's advance. The withdrawal meant, yet again, a dash across open land, and, yet again, there were many casualties.

'B' Company didn't get the order to withdraw and were left behind. The 'B' Company trenches on the left had already been overrun, and enemy fire from the right was intensifying as the Germans got ever nearer their trenches. The situation looked impossible, but there would be no surrender. Major C.A.L. Yate, with just 19 unwounded men, ordered the charge. But before he could make a move, he found himself struggling with German soldiers who had approached him from behind. A few of the KOYLI were bayoneted, but most of them were taken prisoner. They hadn't surrendered but had been overpowered by the German soldiers. The final position to be overrun was Battalion HQ, and resistance, and the Battle of Le Cateau, ended at 4.30pm. Lieutenant-Colonel Bond points out that the *Official History of the Great War* gives 3.30pm as the

---

[70] Op. cit. Bond, p. 726. Sergeant Alfred Walter Patterson, aged 24, son of Major A S and Mrs M J Patterson of 114 Festing Grove, Southsea, Hants. Commemorated on Panel 22A, La Ferté-sous-Jouarre Memorial.

[71] Ibid., p. 727.

end of the battle but did not take into account the final small fight in 'B' Company's trenches.[72]

The 5th Division fell back during the night along the Reumont road and made a halt at the Reumont-Estrées crossroad. What remained of 2/KOYLI were assembled into an adjacent field, where muster was called. Just 8 officers and 320 rank and file answered to their name.[73] The Battalion then marched off with the rest of the 13th Brigade through St Quentin and on to Ollezy, where they were billeted for the night of 27 August. The Battalion was reorganised into just two companies, each with two officers; such were the 2/KOYLI losses in battle. According to Bond, the total losses to the Battalion were 18 officers, 21 Sergeants, 22 Corporals, 7 Buglers and 532 Privates: 600 men in total. Of these, 310 were reported being taken prisoner, including 170 wounded.[74]

The Battalion and the 13th Brigade had succeeded in holding the Germans at Le Cateau whilst the rest of the retreating II Corps put distance between themselves and the Germans. By 29 August, it had broken all contact with the enemy. In a letter sent after the war, the GOC 5th Division, Major-General Sir C. Fergusson, extolled the work of 2/KOYLI at Le Cateau:

'...I am only too pleased to do anything in my power to recognise the behaviour of that Battalion. It was mainly thanks to them that the 2nd Corps was extricated that day, and their stand is historic...'[75]

Historic stand indeed. Five Victoria Crosses were awarded for the action at Le Cateau, with two of them going to 2/KOYLI men: Major Charles Allix Lavington (CAL) Yate of 'B' Company and Lance-Corporal Frederick William Holmes, 'A' Company. The other three were awarded to men of the RFA: Captain Douglas Reynolds, Driver Job Drain and Driver Frederick Luke.

---

[72] Ibid., p. 728.

[73] Op. cit. Edmonds, p. 176.

[74] Op. cit. Bond, p. 729.

[75] Ibid.

Major CAL Yate VC and L/Corporal Frederick Holmes VC

The official accounts of the deeds for which the 2/KOYLI VCs were awarded are as follows:

'Maj. CAL Yate, for conspicuous gallantry and devotion to duty at Le Cateau on August 26th, 1914, in maintaining a vigorous resistance to the last possible moment, refusing all demands to surrender and attempting to charge the enemy when the trenches were being overrun.'

'No. 9376 Lce.-Cpl. F.W. Holmes carried a wounded comrade on his back out of the firing line at Le Cateau under desperate circumstances, and then proceeded to bring a gun team with its gun, which he found limbered up, with all its detachment killed, out of the battle, first with the aid of a trumpeter and finally single-handed.'[76]

The 2/KOYLI War Diary's list of casualties incurred at Le Cateau initially indicated that Major Yate had been killed but was later amended with *'Since reported by War Office as living.'* He had actually been taken prisoner and taken to Targau prisoner of war camp, where he made a number of attempts to escape, finally succeeding on 19 September 1914, but he was spotted by local factory

[76] Ibid., p. 730.

workers and the following day he was quickly apprehended. There is some controversy as to what happened next, but he died that day, aged 42. It was first reported that he had died of his wounds but this doesn't tally with his escape. Some accounts of his death allege that he committed suicide on his capture by slitting his own throat with a razor blade. Having been caught in civilian clothes and being a fluent German speaker, he feared he would be taken for a spy, which probably meant torture and eventually execution. Curiously, the Germans would not allow any of Yate's fellow officer prisoners to see his body nor would they allow them to attend his funeral.[77] He is buried at the Commonwealth War Graves Commission Cemetery in Stahnsdorf near Potsdam.

Major Yate with German soldiers after his capture
(britishbattles.com/first-world-war/battle-of-le-cateau/)

[77] Murland, Jerry, *Retreat and Rearguard 1914 – The BEF's Actions from Mons to the Marne*, Pen & Sword Military, 2014, p. 165.

L/Corporal Holmes survived the war but received a serious wound in the ankle in October 1914 and nearly lost his foot. He returned to active service in October 1915 having been promoted to Sergeant, serving with the 1st Battalion Green Howards. He was later posted to India and awarded a commission with the 9th Battalion Worcestershire Regiment. He was posted to Mesopotamia in July 1917. In early 1918, he suffered a fractured skull in a serious accident and was returned to England. He finally left the army in 1921 as a Captain and migrated to Australia, where he died in 1969, aged 80.

*****

On 28 August 1914, 13th Brigade continued its march towards Paris, passing through Noyon to Pontoise where it bivouacked for the night in a nearby field. The Brigade rested through the next day and resumed its march on 30 August when it crossed the River Aisne at Attichy and made a halt for the night at Faultzy. On 31 August, the march resumed on to Crépy-en-Valois, a trek of some 23 miles. Hungry and exhausted, the Battalion would have been happy to be billeted anywhere. Their experiences of resting so far on the retreat had been basic, usually a bivouac in a field, but this night they were in for an exception to the norm. Their billet for the night of 31 August was described by the Battalion Medical Officer, Lieutenant Cyril Helm, Royal Army Medical Corps, (RAMC), as more accommodating:

'My battalion was billeted in the largest and best-kept farm I have ever seen. The owner was a charming man and showed me all over it, he was extremely proud of his white oxen, which were indeed noble beasts. I tremble to think what probably happened to the place next day when the Huns arrive.'[78]

The following morning, Lt Helm turned the farm into a Dressing Station as the Battalion dug some shallow trenches.

Arthur had been in the thick of the action at Le Cateau and, being a Sergeant, would have had command of at least a platoon, and as casualties amongst the officers and other NCOs mounted, he may well have found himself in command of a larger section of one of the front line trenches.

---

[78] Ibid., p. 139.

Although the Germans were following the 5th Division's retreat, it was not until the morning of 1 September that they came within sight. The 13th Brigade held the outpost line on the right, covering Crépy-en-Valois with the 2/Duke of Wellington's Regiment and the 1/Royal West Kent battalions in the front and the 2/King's Own Scottish Borderers and 2/KOYLI in support. At 6.00am, the German Cavalry came into view and 2/KOSB and 2/KOYLI moved up to the front. However, the Germans attacked the left side of the line but soon withdrew when the guns of the RFA opened up on them. The retirement of the 5th Division resumed, with 2/KOYLI once again in the rearguard.[79]

The 5th Division continued to march, going through Nanteuil and on to Silly where the Battalion was billeted. The following day, 2 September, the Battalion moved on to Cuisy, and on 3 September the River Marne was crossed at Isles-les-Villenoy; billets were found for them at Couilly. At 9.00pm on 4 September, the Division set off again on what was to be a tiresome march through the night until 10.30am on 5 September when they reached Tournan, just 15 miles from Paris. It is here that the great retreat from Mons finally came to an end.[80]

The 2/KOYLI was bivouacked south of the town of Tournan, and it is whilst it was here that much-needed reinforcements arrived by way of 2nd Lieutenant W. Carrington and 80 rank and file, thus bringing the strength of the Battalion up to 8 officers and 512 other ranks.[81]

At 5.10am the following morning (6 September), refreshed and bolstered by their reinforcements, 2/KOYLI was transformed from an army in retreat to a battle-ready force of advance. Marching on to Villeneuve, moving eastwards to outposts, 13 Brigade met with a few German Uhlan scouts in the Forest of Crécy, whom they captured with little resistance. Over the next two days, they marched on to Coulommiers and then reached Boissy-le-Châtel on 8 September. By now, the BEF were on the offensive, approaching and crossing the River Aisne with

---

[79] Op. cit. Bond, p. 730.

[80] Ibid.

[81] There is an obvious discrepancy here with the numbers recorded in the muster taken after the battle: one more officer should make the total 9, and 80 other ranks would increase the number to 400, not 512. It is possible that some of the Battalion were elsewhere in the Division, having lost contact with the Battalion in the confusion of the withdrawal, and did not join their comrades until later. However, this doesn't answer the difference in officer numbers, unless one of them had died of his wounds in the meantime.

the French Fifth Army on one flank and the French Sixth Army on the other; the 13th Brigade was about to engage in the Battle of the Marne.

The 13th Brigade advanced through St Cyr, with the 14th Brigade on their right, pushing the Germans back towards St Ouen. That night (8 September), 2/KOYLI bivouacked near Rougeville, south of the River Marne. Muster was taken, having had 10 stragglers rejoin the Battalion from Le Cateau. The count now showed the strength of the Battalion as being 9 officers and 520 rank & file. II Corps had at this point borne the brunt of the fighting at the two major battles at Mons and at Le Cateau and had sustained over half of the BEF casualties, especially the loss of officers and NCOs.[82]

The advance continued over the Marne on 9 September, with the French Armies driving the Germans back on either side of the British, forcing the Germans facing the BEF to retreat with little resistance, simply to maintain a straight German front. Although the 14th Brigade faced heavy shelling and met with the German Infantry in a defensive position approaching Montreuil, the 13th Brigade's advance continued through to Chezy on 10 September.[83] Further advances were made over the next two days, and, having driven the Germans out of the Serches commune, the Brigade billeted there on 12 September.

On 13 September, a day of heavy rain, the 13th Brigade received orders to take the bridge over the River Aisne at Missy. The West Kents and the Scottish Borderers were to lead the attack, with 2/KOYLI and the 2/Duke of Wellington's Regiment in support. The Germans had established a strong defensive position on the far bank of the river and had destroyed the bridge, making a daylight crossing difficult for the front battalions, which they found to their cost, and the support battalions found themselves the focus of the German Artillery.

The next day (14 September), the two forward battalions waited until nightfall and, using five improvised rafts provided by the Royal Engineers (RE), were able to cross the Aisne in the dark. During the day, at around 1.00pm, 2/KOYLI's position came under enemy shellfire with high explosives. Two men

---

[82] Ascoli, David, *Mons Star – The British Expeditionary Force 1914*, Book Club Associates, London, 1981, p. 160.

[83] Op. cit. Bond, p. 733.

were killed (Private 10618 Walter Francis Clarke[84] and Private 16063 Frank Powell[85]) and five were wounded.[86]

At 1.45am on 15 September, 2/KOYLI advanced to the river with the intention of crossing and supporting the two front-line battalions. When they arrived at the river, they found there was no means to get across: the RE had not built a pontoon bridge, and the rafts were either still on the other bank or had drifted downstream. The Battalion, being exposed and with no way forward, aborted the crossing and retired to a small wood about 400 yards from the river, hopefully out of sight of the German Artillery. This proved not to be the case, and they came under a heavy bombardment. The men were ordered to lie on their stomachs in a single line next to the trees. Lieutenant Cyril Helm takes up the story in his diary:

'We knew we had been seen by the German observers and, almost immediately, four high-explosive 5.9 shells burst together exactly over our heads. They were beautifully timed and only a few yards above us. The scene after that was appalling. A great many men had been killed. My thoughts were indescribable as I realised that, lying on my belly, the next shell might blow me to smithereens.'

Lt Helm describes the groans of the wounded as *'too nerve-wracking for words'*. Lying next to him, his Orderly Corporal was *'frightfully shattered, one of his legs completely blown away. Of course, his death was instantaneous.'*[87]

Death from high-explosive shells could occur from the blast alone, even from a distance, leaving a body intact and as if sleeping, with no physical indication of life extinct. Conversely, a direct hit would disintegrate a body altogether, showering everything and everybody around with a diabolical rain of flesh, brains, blood, and the contents of stomach and bowels. Often, what remained would be quickly buried there and then with little or no ceremony. In moving

---

84 Private 10618 Walter Francis Clarke, born in Peckham, London, commemorated at La Ferté-sous-Jouarre Memorial, Stone number 22.

85 Private 16063 Frank Powell, born in Pontefract, buried at Pontefract Cemetery, Plot M, Grave 1021.

86 2/KOYLI War Diary.

87 From an article by Toby Helm, Cyril Helm's grandson, in *The Guardian*, 3 November 2003.

action of battle, it would be simply left to dissolve into the earth and what was left of the environment, buried and reburied by continuing bombardment. Even intact bodies buried near the front would be disinterred and blown apart by shell blast, the grave becoming a crater.

Cyril Helm also describes the effect of Shrapnel on a young Artillery officer brought to him immediately after being hit:

'The poor fellow was brought into me absolutely riddled. He lay in my arms until he died, shrieking in his agony, and said he hoped I would excuse him for making such a noise, as he really could not help it. Pitiful, as nothing could be done for him except an injection of morphia. I will always remember that incident, particularly as he was such a fine-looking young boy, not more than nineteen.'[88]

The bombardment continued at dawn, with further casualties as the men entrenched as best they could along the front and rear edges of the wood. Their transport mules and horses had bolted, and to make things worse, the weather turned, and their hastily dug trenches soon filled with rain. As there was no way across the river, all they could do was dig in until fresh orders were received. Unsurprisingly, the Battalion was withdrawn at nightfall and was billeted at La Gobinne Wood in the rear, where they remained for a week as the Battle of the Aisne continued. On reaching La Gobinne Wood, they found that nine more officers had been posted to the Battalion.

According to Lt-Col Bond, 2/KOYLI casualties from the German bombardments were 53 killed and wounded.[89] Lt Helm recorded the casualties as 20 killed and about 50 wounded. Seventy per cent of all soldiers killed on the Western Front were the victims of shellfire and mortar bombs.[90]

We are now at a juncture where the two brothers, John and Arthur, would have come together in the Battalion. Having landed in France on 11 September, we must assume that John would have reached the Battalion within a few days. Perhaps he arrived before the above encounter, it being his first action of the Great War. Or he may have spent some time at base camp undertaking some form of induction.

---

[88] Op. cit. Holmes, p. 400.

[89] Op. cit. Bond, p. 734.

[90] Op. cit. Holmes, p. 213.

Either way, for the purpose of this narrative, and with that caveat, in the next chapter I will continue the story assuming that both John and Arthur are sharing the experience as 'brothers in arms'.

John and Arthur Pridmore: Brothers in Arms

Born two brothers loved and lost
Went off to war but at a great cost
Now rest together at peace at last
Our lives were gone way too fast.[91]

Although John and Arthur served in the same Battalion, I had thought it unlikely that they would have fought side by side. They would probably have been in different Companies, certainly not in the same platoon, especially as Arthur was a Sergeant and likely a platoon leader. Having said that, there certainly were occasions where brothers not only served in the same Battalion but were also killed in action on the same day. Three brothers, Arthur, Frank and Frederick Racheil, all served with 3/Royal Fusiliers and were killed at the Battle of Bellewaerde on 24 May 1915. Although they all served in the same Battalion, we don't know if they were in the same Company. Astonishing as this story is, it is not the only one. In fact, there were at least three other instances where three brothers were killed in the same action on the same day on the Western Front, and the Royal Navy lost three Malcolm brothers, Charles, Joseph and John, when H.M.S. *Queen Mary* was sunk on 31 May 1916.[92]
In fact, it was possible for a brother to 'claim' a sibling from another Regiment into his own, a practice continued to this day.[93] However, as John and Arthur both joined the same Battalion, although not at the same time, there was no need for there to have been a 'claim'.

---

[91] Ode to two brothers by Richard Cox

[92] westernfrontassociation.com/world-war-i-articles/brothers-killed-in-action-together

[93] Op. cit. Ascoli, p. 22. See also *Queen's Regulations for the Army*, paras 9.222–9.227

The two Pridmore brothers, along with the rest of the Battalion, had a quiet week following their withdrawal to La Gobinne Wood, and I would like to think that they were able to spend some time together whilst away from the action. Then, on 23 September at 8.00am, there was a conference of commanding officers to discuss plans for attacking the German positions over the River Aisne. At 10.00am the following day, orders were received to relieve the 2/DWR on the north bank of the river. At 1.00pm, the Battalion CO and Company COs did a reconnoitre visit over the river to assess the 2/DWR position. At 8.00pm that evening, the four Companies of 2/KOYLI began to ferry across the river at two-hour intervals. They took up the trenches vacated by 2/DWR, and the following day was spent improving their defensive positions. Further reinforcements arrived on 26 September, bringing the Battalion complement to 21 officers and 780 other ranks.[94]

On Sunday, 27 September, there was relentless shelling of the Battalion's position, culminating with a harsh burst of Shrapnel at around 5.00pm; there were no 2/KOYLI casualties, but there were 5 of 2/KOSB and 3 of 1/RWK. There was intermittent shelling the following two days, but again, no casualties. The highlight of the last day of September was the farewell of the Brigade CO, Brigadier-General Cuthbert, who visited the Battalion on his last day of command before being succeeded by Brigadier-General William Hickie.

It is at this juncture in the War that the German strategy changed. The Battle of the Aisne had reached a bit of a stalemate, and the attention of the Kaiser's new Commander, General Erich von Falkenhayn, turned to taking the Channel ports of Calais and Dunkirk. This new phase of the war became known as the 'Race for the Sea'. II Corps took up position on the right of the BEF in the new Front Line, with the 5th Division on the extreme right of the II Corps line. 2/KOYLI's redeployment from the Aisne trenches took place on 1 October, when they were relieved by 1/Essex at 11.00pm, marching to billets at Vassemy, arriving at 4.00am on 2 October. Later that day, at 6.40pm, the Battalion took to the road again, marching to new billets near Violaine. On 3 October, at 6.40pm, 2/KOYLI marched into billets in Hartennes.[95] The Battalion was on the march over the next four days, with the exception of 5 October, when it stayed billeted

[94] Op. cit. Bond, p. 735. It is worth noting here that although John arrived in France on 11 September, he may not have joined 2/KOYLI's position until later, and maybe not until 26 September.

[95] 2/KOYLI War Diary.

at Lagny. Their long march ended at Verberie on 7 October at 7.00am, where they entrained for Abbeville at 4.00pm, arriving there at 9.15am on 8 October, where they detrained and marched to billets at Drulat. At 6.00pm, they marched off again to Gueschart. More marching on 9 October at 8.00pm, the whole of the 13th Brigade reached Haravesnes about 2.30am on 10 October.[96]

On 10 October, the Battalion spent the day near Villievres, awaiting motor-bus transport to take it to Valhuon. At 4.00pm, the men were all aboard the motor-buses, and they arrived at Valhuon at 6.00pm, where they billeted for the night. At 8.00am the following day, 2/KOYLI set off on the march again to Hesdigneul, where the 13th Brigade were given orders to fill a gap in the line between the French left and the British right. 2/KOYLI went into billets at Vaudricourt.[97]

Motor-buses taking troops to Ypres 1914

At 9.35am 12 October, the 13th Brigade advanced to fill the gap as ordered, with 2/KOSB on the left by a canal, 2/DWR in the centre, and 1/RWK on the right; 2/KOYLI remained in reserve at Annequin. At 5.30am the next day (13 October), 5th Division was ordered to attack all along their line, supported by

---

[96] Ibid.

[97] Ibid.

artillery. By now, the French were supposed to have taken the town of Vermelles but had failed to attack as planned. According to the 2/KOYLI War Diary, this halted the 5th Division's advance.

At about 3.00pm the Germans began a strong counter-attack against the left of 2/KOSB, and 2/KOYLI 'B' Company and a platoon of 'A' Company were sent into the line to reinforce them, with 'C' Company in support. In the action that followed, one man of 'A' Company was killed[98] and one from 'B' Company received only slight wounds.[99] Total casualties for II Corps on 13 October numbered 987.[100]

The fourteenth of October was the day that John Thomas Pridmore was killed in action. Lt-Col Bond simply records that *'the 14th was spent in resisting German counter-attacks',* so I turn to the 2/KOYLI War Diary for a more detailed account of the action.

First, in the early morning, reports were received that the French would not be resuming the offensive at Vermelles, but the day would be spent improving their position; the 13th Brigade were ordered to do likewise. As the Brigade were undertaking the work to improve their defences, the German Artillery opened up with a burst of Shrapnel fire close to the Brigade HQ, and one Signaller was wounded.

At 1.45pm, a message was received informing the Brigade that the French would resume their attack on Vermelles after all, and it would commence at 2.00pm with the support of British Artillery fire. If substantial progress was made by the French, one of II Corps Brigades was to *'endeavour to co-operate'*.

At 3.00pm, orders were received for all 13th Brigade battalions to move to *'co-operate'* at 7.00pm, and that their present positions would be taken over by four French Territorial Battalions. At 3.30pm, further orders were received

---

[98] I have been unable to find any man killed on 13 October in the official list of 2/KOYLI *Soldiers Died in the Great War 1914–19,* but there is one listed as killed in action on 11 October 1914: Private 10837 William Gallagher, commemorated on the Le Touret Memorial, Panel 31. Yet I have been unable to find any reference in my sources to say that a 2/KOYLI man was killed on 11 October; the Battalion was either marching or billeted on 11 October and not in action. I believe the man in question mentioned in the War Diary as killed on 13 October is William Gallagher, despite all records showing that he was killed on 11 October.

[99] Op. cit. 2/KOYLI War Diary.

[100] Op. cit. Ascoli, p. 193.

indicating that a French Division was to make a determined attack on Vermelles and to the north of Vermelles. The French would make their advance through the 13th Brigade's trenches, and the Brigade would support this advance with covering fire until the French had passed through. The four battalions were to remain in their trenches in support until relieved by the French Territorial Battalions.

One of the 2/KOYLI positions was in trenches and in buildings in a village near Pont Fixe—a bridge over the canal—and this area had been subjected to Shrapnel fire throughout the day. A 'B' Company Platoon was forced out of their position in one of the houses in the village due to the concentrated Shrapnel they were receiving; the Germans had identified this particular position for their Artillery's attention. Nevertheless, 'B' Company *'made some excellent practice at some German Infantry trying to cross by a well and by reporting the movement to the Artillery – the whole movement was completely checked.'*

Such Army parlance was typical; associating the killing of enemy infantry with *'excellent practice'*. Just before dusk, further practice was undertaken as a Platoon of German Infantry advanced from the edge of a wood towards the junction of the 2/KOYLI and 2/KOSB trenches. 2/KOYLI 'A' Company was in this position, and the Germans were met with their rifle-fire and that of 2/KOSB. Caught up in this crossfire, the Germans were cut down, and just five of them got back to their own line; excellent practice!

A short time later, just as dusk descended, the Germans attempted another attack at the same point, and they were met by the same crossfire and got no further than 30 yards of the 2/KOSB trenches. One more attack was made at around 7.00pm, but this too was met with the same result; German losses that evening were assumed to be very heavy.

Due to the delayed French attack on Vermelles and its progress, it was expected that the Battalion's relief by French Territorial Battalions would be delayed. And so it was, as it was 4.00am before the trenches were taken over by the French, and 2/KOYLI was able to retire to billets at Le Hamel and once more became Corps Reserve. Bond's narrative of the action on 14 October, sparse though it was, concluded that the Battalion's casualty count was eighteen. The War Diary records the eighteen casualties as: 4 killed, 12 wounded and 2 missing.

On consulting the War Office compilation of 'Soldiers Died in the Great War', six 2/KOYLI infantrymen are listed as having died on 14 October 1914;

five killed in action and one died of wounds.[101] It is likely that at least one of the two listed as missing was also killed. The man who died of wounds may have received his wounds at an earlier date. The six 2/KOYLI infantrymen who died on 14 October 1914 were:

Private 7991 John William Howe, KIA
Private 7869 Harry Jagger, KIA
Private 3/6696 Thomas Jennings, KIA
Private 6640 John Thomas Pridmore, KIA
Lance Sergeant 10177 Ernest Smith, DoW
Private 5706 George Harry Stones, KIA
See Appendix 1 for details about these six soldiers.

---

[101] *Soldiers Died in the Great War 1914–19 – The King's Own (Yorkshire Light Infantry),* originally published by the War Office in 1921, my edition published by J.B. Howard & Son in association with the Imperial War Museum Department of Printed Books, 1989.

Sketch map of the 13th Brigade's position on 14 October 1914[102]

There is no good way to die in war, only some worse than others. As we have already discussed, most soldiers killed in action died from shellfire or mortar bombs. The shells could be high-explosive or Shrapnel; each had its own devastating means of killing.

[102] https://frankcrawshaw.uk/tag/pont-fixe/

I have often contemplated just how my great-grandfather, John Thomas Pridmore, was killed. A clean sniper's bullet that took him instantly, probably the easiest to digest, but, in the circumstances portrayed in the 2/KOYLI War Diary, this end was unlikely. Taking a bullet whilst in action against an advancing German Infantry, still uncomfortable to my mind, was better than him being *'blown to smithereens'*, as Cyril Helm describes death by high-explosive shells, or being riddled with Shrapnel. Yet, shellfire was probably the cause of John's death. This also applies to the other four of his comrades who are recorded as being killed in action that day.

The action that took place at Pont-Fixe on 14 October involved 2/KOYLI fighting from either trenches or from buildings, and had they died from bullets, their bodies would have been retrievable and taken away from the front for burial. Yet only one of them, fellow Sheffield soldier Tom Jennings, has a known grave; he is buried at Brown's Road Military Cemetery at Festubert.[103] All of the others are commemorated on Panel 31 on the memorial at the Le Touret Cemetery, Pas-de-Calais.

Le Touret Memorial (CMGC)

[103] The Commonwealth War Graves Commission records show that 37-year-old Tom had a brother, John W Jennings, living at 23 Cross Bedford Street, Sheffield.

The biographical record for John in *De Ruvigny's* ends with: 'Buried where he fell: *unm*'. Does this mean he was hurriedly buried in a trench and left without ceremony or marker, or any form of record? Or was he atomised by high-explosive and left to the elements?

The bodies of around 100,000 British men have never been identified, including 2,000 from Sheffield.[104] The remains of Great War casualties are still being unearthed in France and Flanders by farmers' ploughs and developers' diggers.

As for the 2/KOYLI men killed on 14 October 1914, we can only consider the possibilities and use our imagination. On the other hand, the man who died of wounds on 14 October, L/Sgt Ernest Smith, does not fit any of these possibilities, unless he was recorded as wounded but died later on the same day.

Under usual circumstances, when a wounded soldier was recovered from the line, after initially receiving emergency treatment, he would be transported to the nearest dressing station behind the line. Had Ernest Smith died at the dressing station, there would be a record of his death, and he would likely have been buried nearby. But again, there is no known grave, and he too is listed on the Le Touret Memorial.

As the battalion wasn't relieved by the French until the early hours of the morning of 15 October, I would have thought there was an opportunity to take the bodies of their fallen comrades, if retrievable, to a suitable burial site and record their details. This doesn't appear to have happened. Or maybe they all lie together in an unmarked mass grave, waiting to be exhumed by the CWGC Recovery Unit.[105]

The BEF, at this early stage of the war, was not prepared for the huge number of casualties, and there were no effective means to deal with them in any form of organised manner. The 1,200 men of the BEF killed at Le Cateau were simply left scattered across the battlefield, as were most of the wounded. I doubt that the Germans would have buried and recorded the dead, as the numbers of their own casualties are not known.

---

[104] Op. cit. Warr, p. 143.

[105] See CWGC website for details about this unit, which recovers around 150 human remains worldwide each year.

Private John T. Pridmore,
K.O.Y.L.I.'s.
Killed in action, 14 October, 1914.

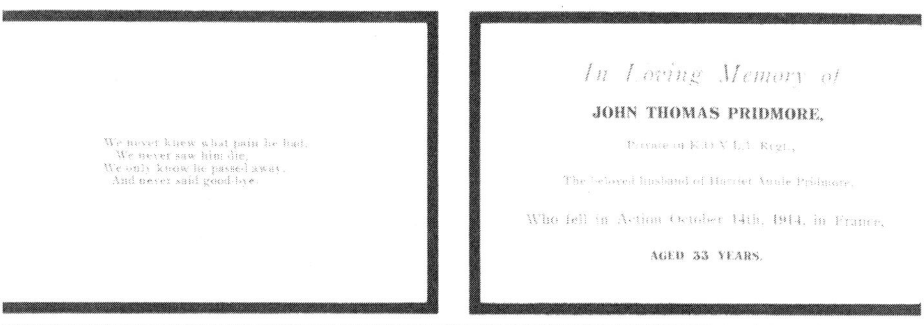

Press photograph of John Thomas Pridmore on the reporting of his death and a family memorial card

Also killed on 14 October was Major-General Hubert Hamilton, CO of II Corps 3rd Division, the first British Army Divisional Commander to be killed in the War. He, too, was killed by a shell fragment whilst surveying the front line. In contrast with the six 2/KOYLI men who died that day, he was buried with a funeral ceremony at Lacouture later that evening, attended by as many officers as could be excused from the line, all of his staff officers, and several II Corps HQ officers. II Corps Commander, General Horace Smith-Dorrien, described the event as:

'...Quite the most impressive funeral I have ever seen or am likely to see – and quite the most appropriate to the gallant soldier and fine leader we were laying in his last resting place. I fancy all were much moved by the scene – as I was myself.'[106]

As the front line moved on, Hamilton's body was exhumed and returned to England, where he was reburied at St Martin's Church in Cheriton, no doubt with more formal military ceremony. The notion, professed by some historians, that the Great War was a class leveller, is a myth; death is a leveller, but when considering the melancholic events of 14 October 1914 above, I don't accept the sentiment.

I can't begin to imagine how Arthur took the death of his older brother. We don't know if he was near to him when he was killed, or if he got the news through the Battalion grapevine. He may have been formally informed by his commanding officer. However the blow was delivered, Arthur had to deal with his emotions whilst keeping his composure; it wouldn't do to let his men see him cry. Or what the hell did it matter? It wasn't the first time grief of this nature had been witnessed within the Battalion; many men had lost brothers or close friends over the last three months. The day after John died, on 15 October, the Battalion spent the day in billets, giving Arthur plenty of time to mull over what had happened. Perhaps it would have been better for him to have to focus on fighting, which would have taken his mind off John's death. Later, in July 1916, Anthony Eden, the future Prime Minister, whilst serving with the King's Royal Rifle Corps (KRRC), was called into Company HQ to be informed of his 16-year-old

---

[106] Op. cit. Beckett, p. 70.

brother, Nicholas Eden, a midshipman on HMS *Indefatigable*, having gone down with the ship on 31 May during the Battle of Jutland. He later recalled that:

> *'It was fortunate for me that during these weeks I was heavily occupied with my two sets of duties as platoon commander and battalion bombing officer, or perhaps thoughtful seniors had arranged it that way. I was overworked, with no time to think.'*[107]

Did 'thoughtful seniors' arrange for Arthur to be too occupied to dwell on John's death? Whether they did or not, tragically, Arthur would have just four days to come to terms with his emotions before he was dealt the same fate.

On 15 October, further reinforcements arrived at the Battalion. The War Diary recorded the arrival of 2nd Lieutenant A.H. Errington[108] and 94 men; it had taken them a month-long journey to get to Le Hamel. On 16 October, the Battalion was ordered to move out at 9.00am to meet up with 1/RWK and then for the two Battalions to join 3rd Division in reserve; 2/KOSB were to stay in 5th Division reserve, 2/DWR were to be joined by the Dorsets and be attached to 13th Brigade Corps Reserve. 2/KOYLI went into billets at Le Touret, then moved again at 2.30pm to Richbourg L'Avour, where they billeted for the night. On this day, the strength of the Battalion was 16 officers and 839 rank & file.

The morning of 17 October brought orders to march again at 9.00am to a point on the map that coincided with the letter 'L' of Pont Logy,[109] where they remained all day waiting for further orders. As the sun set, they went into billets. Then, at 8.30pm, Battalion CO, Brig-Gen Hickie, was ordered to 7 Brigade HQ, from where he sent orders back for 2/KOYLI to march at 2.15am to relieve the Regiment of Irish Rifles at their trenches in front of Lannoy; Arthur would soon be back in action.

---

[107] Eden, Anthony, *Another World*, Penguin Books Ltd, London, 1976, p. 83.

[108] 2/Lt Arnold Henry Parnell Errington was killed in action on 30/31 November 1914. Born 22 June 1885, educated at Haleybury College. He was living in Canada on the outbreak of the War and returned to England to enrol in KOYLI. Commemorated on the Ploegsteert Memorial, Belgium. His medals were auctioned at Noonans Mayfair, 27 June 2002 (£400).

[109] The use of letters of the names of towns and villages on reference maps were often used as location points in War Diaries.

The eighteenth of October was a day of heavy fighting for 2/KOYLI and for heavy casualties. After relieving the Irish Rifles, the Battalion was informed that it would be in the vanguard of a general advance, which would commence at 6.30am, with the Wiltshire Regiment to its right and the Lincolnshire Regiment to its left. However, the Lincolnshire Regiment was relieved by the Scots Fusiliers at the given time, with the same objective: to take Chateau Wood.

At the appointed time, the Battalion moved to the front line with 'C' and 'D' Companies to the fore, with 'A' and 'B' Companies in support. It soon materialised that 2/KOYLI was further forward than the battalions on their flanks, as they both failed to advance any further than 350 yards of the wood due to heavy enemy fire from the edge of the wood and fire from both flanks. 'A' Company went forward in close support, soon followed by 'B' Company and Battalion HQ, which established a base in nearby houses. The Battalion and the rest of the firing line entrenched and took cover as best they could. The line remained under intensive enemy fire, with 2/KOYLI further forward than the battalions on its flanks. There were many casualties, and the wounded were removed to the rear. Sergeant A Macdonald[110] of 'D' Company is given a mention in the War Diary for his action in removing the wounded and returning with ammunition, as is Lieutenant Helm, who had a very busy time treating the wounded, which numbered 70 men that he got away by the evening.

The heavy enemy fire was compounded that evening by tragic events brought about, once more, by poor communications along the line. At around 5.00pm, the Battalion was informed that the Scots Fusiliers, who were on their left, were to attack at dusk with the objective of taking the Fourmes-Illies Road. 2/KOYLI was to conform and to pass the message on to the Wiltshire Regiment on their right. The message didn't get through to 'C' Company, who were on the left of 2/KOYLI, and as the Scots Fusiliers advanced alone, their right flank was immediately exposed and they were soon given the order to retire. In the confusion, one of the Scots platoons lost direction and came back towards the 2/KOYLI trenches, whereupon they opened fire and the Scots were shot down by their own side, a euphemism known as *'friendly fire'*.

---

[110] I believe this to be 6923 Band Sergeant Archibald Boyd Macdonald, DCM & Clasp, Médaille Militaire, who was killed 10 days later on 28 October 1914 at Richebourg L'Avoué, near Béthune, aged 31. His brother, 7281 Lance Sergeant William Gordon Macdonald, also of 2/KOYLI, was killed the following day, 29 October, at Le Touret, aged 24—a sad irony.

The Scots Fusiliers retired about a quarter of a mile, which then left the 2/KOYLI left flank totally exposed, forcing the Battalion also to retire, despite 'D' Company having advanced a few hundred yards. It too had to retire; their efforts and sacrifices all for nothing. The last line in the War Diary for 18 October was the 2/KOYLI casualties for the day: 17 killed and 82 wounded. One of those killed in action was Arthur Edward Pridmore.

Sergeant ARTHUR E. PRIDMORE,
of the K.O.Y.L.I.'S.
Killed in action, 18 October, 1914.

Press photograph of Arthur Edward following his death

On consulting the official list of 2/KOYLI soldiers killed in action on 18 October 1914, I found that the total number is 25. This discrepancy may be due to eight of the 82 listed as wounded in the War Diary having died later in the day. Those who died were:

1. Barringer, Sidney, Private 9272
2. Bartlett, George, Private 7983
3. Bettney, Frederick William, Private 6438
4. Boon, Harry James, Sergeant 6218
5. Cavell, Edward, Private 7135
6. Cross, John Harry, Private 10887
7. Crouch, Percy, Private 6657
8. Currie, William, Private 10676

9. Derham, Joseph, Private 8326
10. Elson, Albert, L/Corporal 9042
11. Gale, George, Private 8534
12. Gollick, George, Private 7932
13. Kelly, John, Private 5877
14. Massey, Robert George, L/Corporal 9273
15. Moody, John Robert, Private 8417
16. Oglesby, Harold, L/Corporal 10868
17. Price, Thomas, L/Corporal 7823
18. **Pridmore, Arthur Edward, Sergeant 7171**
19. Reed, Henry, Private 7790
20. Robinson, Frank Horatio, Private 5866
21. Roebuck, Joseph, L/Corporal 8168
22. Silverwood, Albert, Private 7145
23. Squires, Albert, Private 6975
24. Turner, Percy, Private 10896
25. Willey, William Henry, Private 7165

See Appendix 2 for details about these twenty-five soldiers.

All except four of the 2/KOYLI men listed as died on 18 October 1914 are commemorated on Panel 31, Le Touret Memorial, which suggests that they have no known grave. Three of the other four – Harry Boon, George Gollick and William Willey – are buried in consecutive graves in the Canadian Cemetery No.2, at Neuville-St Vaast. There is no indication that any of them were Canadian. The other – George Bartlett – is buried at Terlincthun British Cemetery at Wimille.[111]

Arthur is recorded as being 'buried *near* where he fell',[112] as opposed to simply 'where he fell'. How do we define the difference? Was he actually buried by his comrades or left on the battlefield? And why were four of the fallen buried in War Cemeteries?

On the day after this action (19 October), the War Diary simply records: *'Nothing much happened all day'*, despite this being the first official day of the

---

[111] Commonwealth War Graves Commission website.

[112] Op. cit. de Ruvigny, Vol.2, p. 140.

First Battle of Ypres (19 October–22 November 1914). One would assume that any retrievable bodies would have been buried and recorded. Perhaps just the four had been retrieved, for if the rest, or at least those whose bodies were retrievable, were buried in a mass grave, the common practice prior to 1914, why weren't they all? What determined that four of them were buried in individual War Cemetery graves?

As with John, we are unable to determine how Arthur met his end, but we can only ponder the possibilities. His wife Annie was living at Bishopthorpe, York, at the time of his death.[113] Back in Sheffield, Thomas and Sarah Pridmore would receive news of the loss of two of their sons within days of each other, just a couple of months or so after the war began. More grief was to follow.

To end this chapter, I want to tell the reader about a most poignant yet bizarre encounter that I had a century after the Great War. In fact, it was on the centenary of the Battle of Le Cateau on 26 August 2014.

Following a letter to the *Royal British Legion* magazine regarding the Pridmore brothers, I was invited to a commemoration of the KOYLI at the Battle of Le Cateau at the Royal Armouries in Leeds by the KOYLI Regimental Association in Yorkshire. The evening began at 7.15pm with a presentation by author and broadcaster Gordon Corrigan on the origins of the Great War, and the events leading up to the Battle of Le Cateau, and the part played by 2/KOYLI. At 8.00pm, there was a quarter-hour bugle call followed by a solo song by L/Cpl Alex Shakespeare of 'E' (Rifles) Company (North & West Yorkshire). There then followed an introduction to the Sounding of Retreat by Lt-Gen T.P. Evans DSO CBE, which was then performed by the Band and Bugles of The Rifles. The evening concluded with a dark suit or blazer dinner for all those invited to the event.

My partner and I entered the dining room and we consulted the information board detailing the seating arrangements, only to find that our names were missing. I enquired with one of the staff as to where we were seated, and we were taken to a table where I sat next to a fellow called Jeff Burdett, who, like me, was a descendant of a 2/KOYLI soldier who had participated in the Battle of Le Cateau. He was there with his mum.

We introduced ourselves and, of course, the subject of conversation was about the evening, which we had both thoroughly enjoyed. Then we talked about

[113] Commonwealth War Graves Commission website.

the soldiers we were there to represent. When I told Jeff that my great-grandfather was killed on 14 October 1914, his jaw dropped, and he told me that the soldier he was there to represent was also killed on 14 October 1914—it was Private John Howe.

Unbelievably, we had been brought together by fate to sit next to each other at the same table at a dinner to commemorate two soldiers from the same battalion who died on the same day, in the same battle, a century ago. For all we know, they may well be lying in the same grave. Jeff later kindly sent me a copy of the 2/KOYLI War Diary, which I have used and found invaluable for this book.[114]

[114] Sadly, Jeff passed away in 2015, and his mum passed away in 2018.

Press photo of Private John William Howe on the reporting of his death (Jeff Burdett)

Le Touret Memorial (Courtesy of George Horner)

Panel 31 Le Touret Memorial (Courtesy of George Horner)

Albert Pridmore

'...had a more tragic Great War than most.'[115]

In Chapter 1, we left Albert Pridmore having moved out of the family home in 1900 and living with his future wife, Margaret May, at 19 Burnt Tree Lane in Netherthorpe. It is here that their first child, Albert Junior, is born on 24 March 1901. At the time that he moved in with Margaret, he was a labourer in a steel works, but later went to work for the Sheffield Corporation (now Sheffield City Council) as a labourer on the roads (1901). In 1903, they moved to House 2, Court 2, Blue Boy Street, and Albert was now working as a builder's labourer, perhaps with his father and brother Ernest. On 16 August 1903, a second son was born: Frederick Pridmore. Sadly, the high rate of Sheffield's infant mortality, discussed earlier, hit the family, as on 19 January 1904, little Frederick succumbed to tubercular meningitis and passed away at home. He was buried at Burngreave Cemetery on 23 January.[116]

Undaunted, on 27 November 1904, Margaret presented Albert with their third child, a daughter: Lily Pridmore. But yet again, tragedy struck the Pridmore family, as Lily became ill, developed bronchial pneumonia, and died of heart failure in the Royal Infirmary on 4 January 1906; she was just 13 months old. She was buried with her brother at Burngreave Cemetery on 8 January. As if these two tragic losses weren't enough for the wider Pridmore family, between the deaths of Frederick and Lily, Ernest Pridmore's second child, Eliza Pridmore, died of measles nephritis at their Shepherd Street home on 30 May 1905, aged

---

[115] Ben Pridmore, in his *Zoomy's Thing* blog – Census Day

[116] Section U2, Grave 110

18 months. She, too, is buried in Burngreave Cemetery on 3 June.[117] To say that the Pridmore family had more than their fair share of infant deaths is an understatement.

Following the death of little Lily, Albert, Margaret and Albert Junior move to House 1, Court 6, Eldon Street, where their fourth child, George Pridmore, was born on 11 January 1907; George would survive infancy and live through two World Wars, dying in 1978.

On 4 November 1908, their fifth child arrived, a boy who they named Ernest after Albert's oldest brother. Ernest, too, was fortunate to survive his early years and lived to the grand old age of 81, ending his days in Havering, Essex. But there was yet more grief ahead for Albert and Margaret.

In 1910, Albert and Margaret moved the family to yet another address, at 27 Matthew Street,[118] where Margaret gave birth to their sixth child on 13 December 1910, another boy, who they name Harold. He lived through the trials and tribulations of childhood in Sheffield and died in May 1972, aged 71.

The census of 1911 informs us that 31-year-old Albert, 29-year-old Margaret and their four surviving children, Albert aged 10, George aged 4, Ernest aged 2 and Harold aged 3 months, are still living at 27 Matthew Street, which we find to be one of Sheffield's many three-roomed houses at the time. Albert is now recorded as a bricklayer's labourer, probably working with his father. Margaret is recorded as 'wife', and their status as 'married', but they didn't actually marry until 22 December 1913, when Margaret was seven months pregnant with their seventh child and living at yet another address, at 54 Brownell Street. It is here that Margaret gave birth to Mary on 5 March 1914, their second, but only daughter to survive infancy and to live a reasonably long life. Mary married one Horace Tomkins on 23 August 1941. She died in March 1993, aged 79 and still in Sheffield.

That Albert and Margaret got married when they did raises the question: why? They had lived together for thirteen years, had had six children, had buried two of them, and had a seventh on the way. They could have married at any time during those years, and they had declared themselves married to the census

---

[117] Section Q, Grave 51

[118] Matthew Street is where one of Sheffield's most tragic incidents of the 19th century occurred in August 1886, when eight children were killed as steel stored against an external wall of Messrs. Daniel Doncaster and Sons caused the wall to collapse into the street where the children were playing. See chrishobbs.com/deathatdoncasters.htm

invigilator twice, with Margaret being recorded as Pridmore. The reason for their decision to marry when they did will remain a mystery, but with hindsight, it was providential for Margaret.

On the declaration of war with Germany in August 1914, the response of the men of Sheffield to enlist in the armed forces was exceptional and immediate. As we have seen, Albert's brother Arthur was already serving and was one of the original BEF to land in France. A second younger brother, John, a veteran of the Boer War, was quick to re-enlist and join Arthur in France & Flanders. His younger brother who was eligible to join the Army, George Harry, had enlisted in January 1914 but wasn't yet on active service. Albert's response to the War was not so hasty. After all, he was 34 years old, and although within the 18-41 age range limit for joining the Army, he may well have thought himself a bit too old. There was no compulsion; joining was entirely voluntary at this time, and perhaps he had higher priorities. After all, he had a wife and five children to support, one a small baby. Whatever his reasons, he resisted the urge to promptly join his brothers in the service of King and country.

Albert's attitude towards joining up may have changed on receiving news of John's death and then, within a matter of days, the news of Arthur's demise. One cannot imagine the emotions that Albert would be feeling at such a time, but what had happened would certainly have played on his mind. George Harry was sure to be sent to France at some point and face the same dangers. Was it this that spurred Albert into eventually enlisting in June the following year? By this time, little Mary was one year old, and Albert Junior had left school and started work on the railways as a wagon greaser, bringing in, if only a meagre wage, added family income. Whatever inspired Albert, he enlisted by joining the 2/4th (Hallamshire) Battalion, York & Lancaster Regiment, a new battalion formed at Sheffield on 21 September 1914.

As if Albert had not had his fair share of grief at this point, having lost two children to disease and two brothers to the War, a further heart-wrenching tragedy was inflicted upon Albert and Margaret just a few months after he joined up.

On the night of Monday, 11 October 1915, 14-year-old Albert Pridmore junior began his second night shift working for the Great Central Railway Company. On completing his first job for the night, having greased a goods train, he returned to a cabin to replenish his grease box so as to grease another train. He was working with another young lad called George Bingley, aged 15. The pair had been warned by a company examiner not to go between wagons but to go round a light engine at the back of the train. Albert had left George working on the train and was reminded by him not to go between the wagons but to go around the train. When George had completed his task, the train began to move, and he saw the flicker of a lamp at the end of the train as it set off. He paid no heed to this, but as Albert had failed to return from the cabin, he went in search of him. He found Albert's body in the six-foot gap between the tracks, and his severed foot between the rails of the four-foot track, and realised it was Albert's lamp that he had seen as the train set off. The young lad had also received severe head injuries. He had apparently been run over by either the train or the light engine; there was no witness to the accident. He was taken to the Royal Infirmary in a Fire Brigade ambulance, where he was pronounced dead by Dr Cobb. A Coroner's Inquest took place on the following Wednesday, where the jury returned a verdict of accidental death, further adding that they thought that young boys who were engaged on the railways at night time, having finished their work, should be escorted back to the cabin by the man under whom they were working.[119] Albert Junior was buried at Burngreave Cemetery.[120]

My research uncovered another mystery here, as there were two other infants buried in the grave in which Albert was interred, with the surname Walden: Mabel Walden, aged 4 months, died in 1899 at 199 Douglas Road, Park Wood Springs; George Walden, aged 9 months, died in 1907 at 141 Fowler Street, Pitsmoor. I have no idea whether there is a family connection with the Waldens, but Albert Senior and Margaret were also later buried in this grave.

It is interesting to note that Albert joined the York & Lancaster Regiment and did not follow his brothers into KOYLI, assuming he had the choice, of course. At the time that Albert enrolled, the 2/4th (Hallamshire) Battalion was a reserve battalion that became part of the 187th (2/3rd West Riding) Brigade of the 62nd (2nd West Riding) Division in March 1915. Its initial role was to supply drafts of replacements to the 1/4th Battalion, which it did until conscription was introduced in early 1916, and the 2/4th Battalion were then mobilised into an active unit. The battalion moved to Nottingham in March 1915 and then to Strensall Common, York, on 10 April 1915; Beverley in July; Gateshead in November; Larkhill in January 1916; Flixton Park in June and finally

[119] *Sheffield Daily Independent*, Thursday, 14 October 1915

[120] Section W, Grave 35

Wellingborough in December 1916. From the battalion War Diary, it appears that a recruiting party were in Sheffield and Rotherham on 5 June 1915. I suspect this is when Albert enrolled at the battalion's Sheffield HQ at Hyde Park. After a period of training, the battalion was sent to the Western Front in January 1917.[121]

Albert Pridmore (author's collection)

At this point, I found another mystery in a report of the *Sheffield Independent* dated 8 August 1916. The caption under the four brothers' photographs indicates that Albert had been wounded. Perhaps he was wounded during training, as George was (see chapter on George Harry), as he too is stated as having been wounded—yet at this point, neither of them had seen action.

[121] longlongtrail.co.uk/army/regiments-and-corps/the-british-infantry-regiments-of-1914–1918/York-lancaster-regiment/

Sheffield Independent

FREE INSURANCE SEE PAGE 2 | TUESDAY, 8 AUGUST, 1916 | ONE HALF-

OUR MEN OF DEEDS.

Sergeant A. E. Pridmore (1), killed. Private W. T. Pridmore (2), killed. Private A. Pridmore (3), wounded. Corporal G. H. Pridmore (4), wounded. These brothers were the sons of Mr. and Mrs. Pridmore, 31, Hunt street.

A GENTLEMAN'S OVERCOAT

Designed by a master and cut and made by experts, Kenneth Durward Coats are no ordinary ready-made garments. As sole agents for Sheffield we are now showing a fine range in light-weight

Sheffield Independent, 8 August 1916

The 2/4th (Hallamshire) Battalion, York & Lancaster Regiment (2/4Y&LR) embarked on three boats at Southampton on Saturday, 13 January 1917, disembarking at Le Havre the following day. On Monday, 15 January, it entrained for Frevant, arriving there the following day (the French rail system doesn't appear to have improved since 1914). On arrival at Frevant, the Battalion marched to Barly, where it billeted on French soil for the first time. The Battalion stayed in Barly until Monday, 22 January, from where it marched to Candas, staying overnight, and then marched on to Famechon on 23 January.

The first two days at Famechon were spent digging trenches for practice attacks, a job not made easy by the frozen ground. This was the coldest winter on record in Europe at the time. The cold also affected the men, many suffering from exposure; it was a far cry from the warm billets that they left in England.

The attack exercises took place the following day, involving the other three infantry battalions of the 187th Brigade: 2/5Y&LR, 2/4KOYLI and 2/5KOYLI.[122] The War Diary notes that, following the exercises, *'many minor*

[122] *2/4Y&LR War Diary.* Also included in 187th Brigade were the 208th Machine Gun Company and the 187th Trench Mortar Battery, but there is no mention of them having taken part in this exercise.

points require attention.' It would appear that the officers didn't think the Battalion was ready to take on the Germans at this point.

On 29 January, the Battalion was detailed for railway construction, with 'A' and 'C' Companies near Authie and 'B' and 'D' Companies near Sarton; not the sort of work that Albert and the new recruits to Kitchener's New Army would have been expecting on taking up arms. Whenever the infantryman wasn't in the trenches, he would always be found with work to do, often more arduous than being in the firing line; there is more to fighting a war than the use of a rifle and bayonet.

Working Party on Arras Railway Work (Imperial War Museum)

The strength of the 2/4Y&LR Battalion at the end of January 1917 was 36 officers and 981 other ranks, including an interpreter.

The first week of February 1917 was a period of more training, and Box Respirators were issued on 3 February; the Germans had used poison gas for the first time in April 1915. On 4 February, a Brigade School was formed under 'C' Company Commander Major J.W. Richardson[123] for the instruction of junior

---

[123] Major John Watson Richardson, aged 34, son of Mr S G Richardson of Stone Grove, Broomhall, Sheffield, was killed in action on 3 May 1917, shot in the head by a German sniper. He is commemorated at Arras Memorial.

NCOs, but this was cancelled on the following day after orders were received to prioritise the railway construction work over all other work and training.

One training session involved a 24-hour spell in the trenches for a party of NCOs and a number of 'specialists': 8 Bombers, 7 Lewis Gunners and 3 Signallers. This first experience in the trenches resulted in no casualties for the Battalion. These sessions at the front ceased on 6 February, but the following day, verbal instructions were received to the effect that the Battalion would take over part of the line in a few days' time. However, this was cancelled the next day. Was this down to the Battalion still not being ready for action in the eyes of the commanding officers?

The cold weather continued to hamper the work on the railway, and a number of men were evacuated to the Casualty Clearing Station (CCS), suffering from exposure.

On 16 February, the Battalion moved to Bertrancourt, billeting for the night, from where 'A' and 'C' Companies were detailed to move to Auchonvilliers on the 17th to undertake work on a tramway. On 19 February, the Battalion was ordered to take up a position on the Front Line at Beaumont Hamel. The next day, 2/4Y&LR relieved 2/5th West Yorkshire Regiment in reserve, occupying dugouts previously used by the Germans during the prelude to the Battle of the Somme of 1916. By now, there was no regular system of trenches, only dugouts and shell-holes, and the nature of the ground made it difficult for the transport of food and ammunition supplies. The War Diary noted that *'this is a severe test for a Division which has not previously been tested in trench warfare under active service conditions.'* This suggests that there were still doubts about the Battalion's readiness for action.

The Battalion finally moved into the firing line on 22 February, relieving 2/5KOYLI, who reported that it had suffered much annoyance from an enemy sniper, having wounded two of their officers. This sniper wasn't long in annoying 2/4Y&LR, who held the line until the evening of 24 February. Captain William Newlyn Gale[124] had a *'most miraculous escape'*, his revolver saving his life by deflecting the sniper's bullet from the side of his body to his forearm, which sustained a flesh wound. However, the Battalion got the better of this German sniper soon after this incident, when Private 3255 Wycherly turned his

---

[124] Captain William Newlyn Gale was killed in action on 3 May 1917, at Bullecourt; he was last seen pushing forward in front of his men and it is believed that he was blown to pieces by an enemy shell. He is commemorated at Arras Memorial, Bay 8.

machine gun over an area where he had spotted a slight movement. A short while after this burst of fire, a reconnaissance party found the body of the sniper with a number of bullet wounds to the head; the body was still warm when found.

At 3.15pm on 24 February, instructions to advance at 4.00pm were received from Battalion HQ. The passing of instructions to the most advanced posts was delayed until 3.50pm. It is at this point in the record that mention is made again about the difficulties in getting supplies forward to the troops in the firing line, and that *'the men holding advance posts had been without food and water for 12–24 hours, which was due to the great difficulties in getting to them.'*[125] The Battalion moved off with 'D' Company on the right, 'C' Company on the left and two platoons of 'B' Company in the centre; 'A' Company was in support behind 'C' Company, with the rest of 'B' Company supporting 'D' Company. The Battalion advanced without making contact with the Germans by the time darkness fell. At this point, the advance halted and the Battalion consolidated the line, making contact with the South Staffordshire Regiment on their left, but it failed to make contact with the 63rd Division on their right, as instructed. During the night, the Battalion was informed that the ground they had won would be taken over by 2/4KOYLI; it was relieved at 5.00am, 25 February, and returned to dugouts near Beaumont Hamel. On this day in the Diary, it is pointedly recorded that 2/4Y&LR were the first Battalion of the 62nd Division to be sent forward against the enemy, this, whether they were ready or not.

As with John and Arthur, we have no way of knowing which Company Albert was in. All we can do is imagine the possibilities and speculate on his activities. He was in one of them, and he was involved in this first advance of the 62nd Division, although the Battalion had now been in France for two months and had yet to engage the enemy in battle. The only casualties thus far were men suffering from the freezing conditions. It wouldn't be long before that changed.

On the following day, the Battalion moved to Lytham Camp near Maillet-Mailly, where it stood at rest for the next week. Its next orders arrived on 4 March. These were to move into dugouts at Bois D'Holland, where 2/4Y&LR would support units of the 185th Brigade in the line there. The Battalion would also come under the orders of the General Officer Commanding 185th Brigade, which consisted of four Battalions of the West Yorkshire Regiment (WYR). The Battalion moved into line the next day, 5 March, relieving 2/5WYR in a two-

[125] *2/4Y&LR War Diary.*

company frontage: 'C' and 'D' Companies in the line, 'A' Company in support and 'B' Company in reserve. This line was held until the night of 7 March.

During 6 March, a strong patrol, including a Lewis Gun Section and two Bombing Sections (from 'C' and 'D' Companies), was sent out to ascertain the condition of the wire in front of Achiet-le-Petit. The patrol moved forward in file and, after around 400 yards, encountered a German patrol of similar size, which opened fire on them. Despite the patrol rushing the Germans, the enemy soldiers managed to get away. During this encounter, two of the men, Private 2855 G. Frost of 'D' Company and Private 5175 H. Cowling of 'C' Company, were wounded. Private Frost subsequently died.[126] The patrol returned without achieving its objective. There were five other 2/4Y&LR men wounded on 6 March, presumably in exchanges on the firing line: one Sergeant, one Lance Corporal and three Privates.

As expected, the Battalion was relieved by 2/4KOYLI on the night of 7/8 March, and it withdrew to dugouts near Miraumont, where it was heavily shelled by German Artillery, killing one man, Private 4861 Westby Street,[127] and wounding four others, all Privates.

On the following day, 9 March, the Battalion went back in the line, relieving 2/4KOYLI: 'A' and 'B' Companies in the line; two platoons of 'D' Company in support and 'C' Company in reserve with the other two platoons of 'D' Company. The Battalion maintained this position in the line until 15 March. Eleven men were wounded on 10 March, including an officer, Lieutenant R.E. Main-Price. The rest consisted of one Sergeant, one Lance Sergeant, one Lance Corporal and seven Privates.

On 11 March, Battalion HQ received heavy shelling, but there were no casualties. During that night, another patrol went out, led by Captain C.E. Stuart,

---

[126] Private G. Frost, aged 27, was born in Swinton, Rotherham, son of the late John and Ester Frost. He is buried at Queens Cemetery, Bucquoy, Grave I.F.7. I have found no Christian name for G. According to CWGC records, his service number was 200980. This is due to a change in service numbers for all Territorial Force Infantrymen as of 1 March 1917, following Army Council Instruction 2414 of 1916. This isn't helpful for the researcher.

[127] Private Westby Street, aged 20, was the son of William Henry and Ellen Street of 116 Slinn Street, Crookes, Sheffield. He too is buried at Queens Cemetery, Bucquoy, Grave I.F.1. Again, CWGC gives a different service number to that in the 2/4Y&LR War Diary: 202535 (see note above).

and once again met with an enemy patrol. This exchange resulted in the capture of one of the Germans, with no casualties.

On the following night, at around 11.00pm, Captain Stuart led another patrol to establish a new line of advance posts, but this time it was met by enemy machine-gun fire, forcing the men to withdraw, with Captain Stuart being severely wounded and two men missing: Private 2941 Frederick Henry Harrison[128] and Private 5142 Horace Bellairs.[129] It was thought that Horace Bellairs had been killed and Henry Harrison taken prisoner, but in fact they had both been killed.

Back in the line, the Battalion suffered further casualties on 12 March: two killed and seven wounded. Two others also died of their wounds this day. Those killed were Lance Corporal 17213 George Ellis Holgate[130] and Private 5340 George Henry Critchell.[131] Those who died of their wounds were Private 5226 A. Roberts[132] and Private 5278 Charles Henry Moore.[133]

---

[128] Private Frederick Henry Harrison, aged 19, son of Walter and Alice Harrison of 190 Ellesmere Road, Pitsmoor, Sheffield. He is buried at Gommercourt British Cemetery No.2, Hebuterne, Grave v.k.18. CWGC record his service number as 201050.

[129] Private Horace Bellairs is commemorated at Theipval Memorial, Panel 14A and Panel 14B. CWGC record his service number as 202560. There is no further information available.

[130] Lance Corporal George Ellis Holgate, aged 25, son of John Herbert and the late Mary Holgate of Hanley, Stoke-on-Trent. CWGC record his service number as 204372 and rank as Private. He is buried at Gommecourt Wood New Cemetery at Foncquevillers, Grave I.A.3.

[131] Private George Henry Critchell, aged 32, son of Joseph and Elizabeth Critchell. CWGC record his service number as 202732. He is buried at Gommecourt Wood New Cemetery at Foncquevillers, Grave I.C.26.

[132] I have found no Christian name for Private A. Roberts (recorded in War Diary as J. Roberts but no matches on CWGC site). CWGC record his service number as 202633. He is buried at Varenne Military Cemetery, Grave No. I.J.24. A contact name on the grave headstone information form is Mrs M.J. Burmah of 69 Attercliffe Road, Sheffield.

[133] Private Charles Henry Moore is commemorated at Theipval Memorial, Panel 14A and Panel 14B. CWGC record his service number as 202681. There is no further information available.

Further casualties were recorded on 13 March, with one fatality: Corporal 3231 John Thomas Richardson.[134] Of six men listed as wounded, one was suffering from shell shock and another having been gassed. Amongst the wounded was Captain H.E. Jenkinson. The Battalion was relieved by the 2/5th Duke of Wellington's Regiment on 15 March and went into rest at Puisieux, with instructions to move to Forceville on the following day. Just one wounded was recorded on 15 March.

On 17 March, 'D' Company moved to Lealvillers, with the rest of the Battalion staying in their billets at Forceville. On the 19th, 'A' Company was detailed to move to Englebelmer to undertake 'salvage work', whilst the rest of the Battalion moved into dugouts back at Beaumont Hamel, where the men would resume work on railway construction. On the 21st, 'B', 'C' and 'D' Companies moved to Miraumont, still engaged in railway construction, as 'A' Company remained in Englebelmer, continuing its salvage work. Thus the Battalion remained for the rest of March, during which time Captain Stuart died of his wounds and the body of Private Henry Harrison was found by a search party in the area where he was presumed to have been captured.

On 31 March, the Battalion received reinforcements of seven officers: two Captains, one Lieutenant and four 2nd Lieutenants.

April saw the Battalion continuing its railway and salvage work, with 'B', 'C' and 'D' Companies moving from Miraumont to Achiet-le-Grand on the 4th, where their work on railway construction ceased, though they were still assigned to the Railway Transport Officer (RTO). 'A' Company were still on salvage work at Englebelmer, but rejoined the Battalion the next day. It continued working for the RTO on the 6th.

---

[134] Corporal John Thomas Richardson, aged 33, son of the late Robert and Sarah Richardson, husband of Elizabeth Richardson of 178 Staniforth Road, Attercliffe, Sheffield. CWGC record his service number as 201283. He is commemorated at Thiepval Memorial, Panel 14A and Panel 14B.

Railway construction at Arras 1917 (Imperial War Museum)

Private Albert Pridmore (Courtesy of Paul Pridmore)

Throughout the next three days (7–9 April), the Battalion undertook training exercises, practising attacks as per the *'Instructions for the Training of Divisions in Offensive Action'*. The 10th and 11th were spent moving from camp to Sapignes and back (10th), then Behagnies and back (11th). No reasons for these manoeuvres are given in the War Diary, but I assume it was all part of the training programme. It is worth noting at this point that 9 April was the official start date of the Battle of Arras, which played out until 16 May; the 187th Brigade played its part in this battle, which, although a shorter battle than that of the Somme of 1916, was more costly in daily casualties, averaging just over 4,000 casualties per day, in contrast to around 3,000 during the Battle of the Somme. However, it is the devastating number of casualties on the first day of the Battle of the Somme (1 July 1916) that people have difficulty computing: 57,470, of which 19,240 were killed.

The Battalion moved to Mory on 12 April, where the men's work duties were put under the command of Company Commanders for the next three days; whatever these duties were, they are not recorded in the War Diary, but it is likely to have been further training. However, it is recorded that on the 15th, twelve men of 'A' Company were accidentally wounded by defective bombs, probably whilst training; such accidents were not rare occurrences during the War.

On 16 April, the Battalion was engaged in more construction work, repairing roads around Mory and filling mine craters; the roads had been affected by the severe frost as well as shellfire. This would be something that Albert was used to, since his civilian jobs were builder's labourer and working on Sheffield's roads.

On 18 April, three officers and three men of 'D' Company were wounded; there is no explanation as to how, but possibly from artillery fire or perhaps another accident in training. The Battalion moved camp to Ervillers on this day, where, for the rest of April, it continued training for a forthcoming offensive, including night attacks. Another man, Private Marshall of 'C' Company, was wounded on the 19th' and four more officers joined the Battalion before the month was out. By 1 May, the Battalion's strength was 41 officers and 804 other ranks.

On 2 May, the Battalion was notified that this was 'Y' Day; 'Z' Day being the day of the offensive and the day of the start of the big push that they had been training for. The 62nd Division was to attack the Hindenburg Line in conjunction with the 1st ANZAC Corps. The objective of 2/4Y&LR was the first and second line of German trenches opposing its designated part of the line. Battalion objectives were allotted by Company: 'A' and 'C' Companies were tasked with taking the first German trench line, 'B' and 'D' Companies were to move forward over the first trench line and through 'A' and 'C' Companies to occupy the second (reserve) German trench line. The War Diary details just how this would be achieved, but such military minutiae of line, formation and coordinates should not trouble us. The narrative goes on to state that the battalion was '*in good spirit and that every man appeared to know what was required of him.*'

At 6.45pm, the Battalion paraded in close column of platoons and the CO, Lieutenant-Colonel F. St J Blacker, read out an address from the Divisional Commander, Major-General W.P. Braithwaite:

'As the Division will shortly be going into action to take part in its first great battle, the Divisional Commander desires to assure all ranks of his complete confidence in their ability to defeat the German troops opposed to them. That the 62nd (West Riding) Division will maintain its reputation for Staunchness and Grit – qualities for which Yorkshiremen have ever been famed – that they will gain all objectives and hold them against the most determined counter-attacks, is the firm conviction of the General Officer who is proud to be their commander.'

Following the address, the Battalion moved off towards their next position near St Leger, where they had a hot meal served from the Field Kitchens; the officers had their supper in a ruined house, where they synchronised their watches and were informed by the CO that 'Zero hour' was 3.45am, 3 May, and final arrangements were made for the offensive.

At 10.15pm, the Battalion paraded again and moved off to the rendezvous point at the crossroads at St Leger, arriving at 10.45pm. From there, it marched to a designated mine crater on the Croisilles-Ecoust St Mein road. At this point, the signallers, runners, stretcher bearers and carrying party branched off and proceeded to Battalion HQ. The rest of the Battalion, Machine Gun Corps and Trench Mortar Battery continued to move forward along the road to an agreed point, where it met with the Brigade Major before moving to their 'tape lines',[135] from where they would go into action.

However, at this point, the Battalion came under enemy shellfire, and Albert Pridmore's war came to an end as he and five other men were wounded in the bombardment; they would not participate in the Battalion's first great battle; nor would they participate in what the *Official History of the War* called the *'blackest* [day] *of the war'.*[136]

This ill-conceived offensive covered sixteen miles of the Front Line from the Vimy-Acheville road in the north to Bullecourt to the south. Between 9 April and 17 May 1917, 4,233 men of 62nd Division were killed in action;[137] 162 on 3 May. 2/4Y&LR casualties on 3 May were: 4 officers and 6 other ranks killed; 4 officers and 130 other ranks wounded; 18 other ranks missing, believed killed; 18 other ranks wounded and missing; and 57 other ranks missing, 237 casualties in total, recorded in the War Diary.

During 3 May and early 4 May, the Battalion Medical Officer, Captain Sharrard, RAMC, dealt with about 80 casualties at the Regimental Aid Post (RAP).

German prisoners moving British casualties at Arras (Imperial War Museum)

---

[135] 'Tape lines' were designated lines from where an attack would commence. The line was marked by lengths of white tape, hence 'tape line'.

[136] Nicholls, Jonathon, *Cheerful Sacrifice – The Battle of Arras 1917*, Pen & Sword Military, Barnsley, 2015, p. 196.

[137] Ibid., p. 224.

The responsibility for getting the wounded away from the Front Line, and for their subsequent care, lay with Captain William Sharrard. The casualty chain began with the wounded man being stretchered to the Regimental Aid Post, which was run by Captain Sharrard. The Battalion had 32 stretcher bearers at this point, and at least six men would be needed per stretcher.[138]

Throughout the War, the ratio of stretcher bearers to fighting men was 32 per 1,000.[139] Prisoners of War would often be drafted in as stretcher bearers to carry the wounded back to the RAP, where responsibility for the wounded man would then be handed to the Royal Army Medical Corps (RAMC) Orderlies. After initial treatment, the patient would be transferred to the Advanced Dressing Station (ADS), either by foot if the man was able, by stretcher, or by cart; in Albert's case, it is unlikely that he was able to walk. From the ADS, he would be moved to the Main Dressing Station (MDS), usually by horse-drawn or motorised Field Ambulance (FA), which would be beyond the range of medium artillery fire. From there, he would be transported to the Casualty Clearing Station (CCS), which was beyond the artillery zone. Here, operations would be carried out on the soldiers who needed them. Many died on the operating table or whilst waiting for the surgeon. These bodies were buried nearby, and many of these impromptu cemeteries later became Commonwealth War Grave cemeteries.[140]

Finally, if he was unlikely to return to active service any time soon, he would be transported to one of the General or Stationary Hospitals, located near railway lines to facilitate movement of the wounded, but still within the theatre of operations. The last link in this chain was a 'ticket' for transportation to England on a hospital ship; these soldiers would have what was known as a 'Blighty' wound.

Such would have been Albert's experience, and once back in England, he was taken to Bradford Military Hospital, which is another mystery of the Pridmore brothers' story: why Bradford and not Sheffield? After all, there were plenty of hospitals in Sheffield adapted for the return of wounded soldiers, and the Third Northern General Hospital was established on Ecclesall Road as a

---

[138] Doyle, Peter, *The British Soldier of the First World War,* Shire Publications Ltd, 2014, pp. 36–37.

[139] Lewis-Sempell, John, *Six Weeks – The Short and Gallant Life of the British Officer in the First World War,* Weidenfeld & Nicolson, 2010, p. 283.

[140] Ibid., p. 286.

military hospital in 1914, specifically for Sheffield's wounded soldiers. Perhaps they were all at capacity at this time; it was a period of high casualties on the Western Front. Or perhaps it was because of Albert's specific medical needs, which required specialist treatment not available at Sheffield but was available at Bradford, yet I have been unable to establish any form of relevant specialism at Bradford Hospital.

Albert's determined hospital is more likely to be due to available capacity at the time. Without knowing the nature of his wounds, or the capacity situation at the time, neither of which I have been able to ascertain, this remains a mystery. Being a survivor of shellfire, it is most likely to have been catastrophic flesh wounds. These could possibly have been made worse by contamination from the battlefield, such as mud and whatever else was flying around in the blast, which could cause infection.

Whatever wounds they were, they were to prove fatal, as Albert Pridmore died in Bradford Hospital on 22 June 1917. His body was brought back to Sheffield and buried with his son, Albert Junior, at Burngreave Cemetery. He is commemorated on the War Memorial Screen at Burngreave Cemetery.

THE SHEFFIELD DAILY INDEPENDENT, TUESDAY, 26 JUNE, 1917.

PRIDMORE.—In ever loving memory of our dear son and brother, Pte. A. Pridmore, who died on June 22nd from wounds received in action on May 2nd, 1917; also of his brothers, Sergt. A. E. Pridmore and Pte. J. T. Pridmore, who were killed in action on Oct 14th and 18th, 1914.
—From their Father and Mother, Brothers and Sisters, also Sister-in-law.

Newspaper memorial for Albert and his brothers from his family

War Memorial at Burngreave Cemetery

George Harry Pridmore

'He was a gallant and conscientious officer,
who knew his work well and was liked by his men.'[141]

When George Harry Pridmore left school in 1910, he started his working life as an errand boy for James F. Eardley, Pharmaceutical Chemist & Mineral Water Manufacturer at 265 Glossop Road, Sheffield. Eardley also had outlets at 59 Upper Hanover Street and 283 Fulwood Road, with a factory at Ecclesall Mineral Water Works at 65 Stalker Lee Road. James Eardley lived at 14 Broomhall Road.[142] It is clear to see from this network why he would employ an errand boy. George then moved to George Cooper and Sons (Sheffield) Ltd, nuts and bolts manufacturers at 147 Leveson Street, Effingham Road, working as a labourer. James Gould, manager at George Cooper and Sons, gave George a character reference when he applied to join the Army on 12 January 1914, stating that he was a fair worker. George's second referee appears to have been his barber, David Pilmore junior of 191 St Phillips Road, who declared himself a Hairdresser by profession; David Pilmore senior was also a Hairdresser at 25 Scotland Street.[143]

---

[141] Obituary by his Major.

[142] *White's Directory of Sheffield and Rotherham*, 1911, Kelly's Directories Ltd, Sheffield.

[143] Ibid.

1911 Advertisement for George’s employer: George Cooper & Sons Ltd

It is clear that George was keen to follow his brothers into the Army, for he applied to join at the earliest possible time that he could; he was aged 17 years and 204 days. He had a job, albeit not one that paid a lot, but at least he was employed. He wasn’t desperate for work, as many recruits to the Army were at the time, but he was desperate to join the Army.

From his attestation medical statement, we find that George Harry was 5’ 5⅞”, weighed 120lb, had a chest size of 35½”, 39” expanded and had a good pulse rate. He had brown hair and bluish-grey eyes. There are also recorded slight physical defects, but not sufficient to cause rejection: knock-knee and scoliosis (spinal deformity), and he was pigeon-breasted. Distinguishing marks were a scar to his right breast and to his forearm. Major F. Winslow RAMC considered him fit for the Army Reserve. And like his two brothers before him, he joined the 3rd Battalion King’s Own Yorkshire Light Infantry – Special Reserve – and became Private 3/1334, signing up for six years.

His first six months as a Special Reservist were spent in basic training at Pontefract, where he gained a 3rd Class Certificate on 29 January and a 2nd Class Certificate on 26 February. This basic training was for physical fitness, drill, marching discipline and essential fieldcraft.

At the outbreak of the War, 3/KOYLI was mobilised (5 August 1914) and moved to Hull as part of Britain’s coastal defences. George Harry must have made a good impression, as on 14 September 1914, he was promoted to Lance-Corporal and, despite being severely reprimanded and forfeiting 7 days’ pay for being absent (I can't make out details) from 31 December 1914 to 6 January 1915, he was promoted to Corporal on 22 January 1915.

This first reprimand was followed by three more during 1915, all for overstaying his pass: 24 May, 25 August and 8 November. Each time he also forfeited pay: 2 days, 1 day and 8 days respectively. The 8-day pay forfeiture, along with a severe reprimand, was for overstaying his pass for 7 days; it is surprising that he wasn't demoted for this, but we don't get to know why he was absent for so long.

Although the first of these unofficial absences was over the Christmas period, I think the reason for his actions may have been due to being informed of the death of his brothers and that he went to Sheffield to be with his family. Although John and Arthur had been killed in October, as with all deaths in the Army, there were a series of inquiries and a waiting period before their next of kin were informed. It probably took longer in the early period, especially if at a time of many casualties after major battles. It may well have been December before the family was officially informed.

Corporal George Harry Pridmore, 1 December 1915 at Hull

George stayed with 3/KOYLI through 1915 before moving to 2/KOYLI, Service Battalion, once more following in the footsteps of his fallen brothers. On

4 May 1916, he was posted to France but didn't embark until 15 December at Folkestone, disembarking later that day at Boulogne. This delay will have been due to him being wounded, probably during training. His medical records show that on 4 July 1916, he was admitted to Third Southern General Hospital at Oxford with a gunshot wound to his hand and fingers. He was moved to Burton Court Hospital, Kintbury, Berkshire, on 12 July, where he stayed until 31 July; a total of 27 days in hospital. Once discharged from hospital, there would have been a period of convalescence, and he would then have to satisfy Army doctors that he was fit for active service. The process of posting to France would then have to begin again.

Like all who went to France subsequent to the original British Expeditionary Force (BEF) of 1914, George was posted to Étaples, where he joined the rest of 2/KOYLI and began intensive training in readiness for combat. On 10 January 1917, he was posted to 8/KOYLI, one of the new battalions which was formed in September 1914 and went to Belgium in August 1915. He joined this battalion in the field on 27 January 1917. This meant he had missed the Battle of the Somme, where 8/KOYLI casualties were one of the greatest on the first day, 1 July 1916. All officers, except the Medical Officer, were killed (10) or wounded (14), and only 110 of the 659 other ranks presented themselves at muster after the battle. Of the other ranks' casualties, 35 were killed, 122 were missing and 365 were wounded and managed to reach the dressing stations.[144]

By the time George joined the battalion, it was on duty in the Ypres sector in Corps Reserve at Montreal Camp at Ouderdom, near Vlamertinghe. He arrived days after one of the Battalion Companies ('D') had raided the German line on 23 January. This was a successful raid, but again, there were many casualties. All three officers involved were wounded, as were 49 other ranks, and 8 other ranks were killed. Two of the officers received the Military Cross for their actions during this raid: Captain H. C. H. Bull and Second Lieutenant H. A. Dinsdale. Sergeant M. White received the Distinguished Conduct Medal.[145]

When George arrived and reported to Battalion HQ on 27 January 1917, the men were either on working parties or training and remained on these details for the rest of January.[146] He would be assigned to the Battalion's 'A' Company. During these four days, there was much to-ing and fro-ing of battalion officers.

---

[144] Op. cit. Bond, p. 820.

[145] Ibid., p. 861.

[146] *8/KOYLI War Diary.*

On the day he arrived, one Second Lieutenant went to hospital (no mention of being wounded, so must have been sick). On the following day, another 2nd Lt went to hospital, a captain left the battalion for a training course, another 2nd Lt returned from a training course and one transferred to the Royal Flying Corps (RFC) as an Observer, another 2nd Lt took over command of 'C' Company and yet another 2nd Lt was put under close arrest; no indication as for why. On 30 January, the battalion mess hut burnt down and the battalion had gas-attack practice at 'Gas School.' Then, on the final day of January, whilst training continued, the X Corps Commander, General Sir Thomas Lethbridge Napier Morland, paid a visit and the 2nd^d Lt under close arrest was put under open arrest; probably to save awkward questions. Another 2nd Lt moved to Machine Gun Corps, and a Captain died of his wounds: Cpt Malcolmson Gardiner Donahoo.[147] By now, George must have thought he had joined Pablo Fanque's Circus.

On 1 February, 8/KOYLI relieved 11th Battalion West Yorkshire Regiment in Brigade Reserve at Ypres Infantry Barracks and remained there until 6 February, undertaking further training and providing working parties. On the 6th, the battalion relieved the 8th Battalion York & Lancaster Regiment in the trenches, and 8/KOYLI HQ moved into Dormy House at Zillebeke. On the 9th, it was relieved by 8/Y&LR and moved back into Brigade Reserve, having had a quiet few days in the trenches, with just Battalion HQ being shelled at 5.00pm on the 7th. Further training and work parties occupied the men until 13 February, when they exchanged positions with 8/Y&LR in the trenches once more.

[147] Captain Malcolmson Gardiner Donahoo, aged 43, son of Thomas Malcolmson Donahoo and Anna E.M. Donahoo, husband of Annie Donahoo of The Cottage, Wonersh, Guildford. Buried at Lijssenthoek Military Cemetery, Grave X.A.2.

Men of the West Yorkshire Regiment in a shell-hole near to the Ypres Infantry Barracks, 23 December 1917 (Imperial War Museum)

The Battalion was next relieved from the trenches by the 12th Battalion Durham Light Infantry on the evening of 17 February. The exchange with 12/DLI in the trenches was completed at 5.30am on the 18th, and the Battalion then marched back to Montreal Camp at Ouderdom, where it went back into Corps Reserve, the last platoon arriving at 9.00am. Further training and small work parties were the order of the next six days at Corps Reserve, until being relieved by the 12th Battalion Royal Sussex Regiment on 24 February, then marching to Bollezeele, where the Battalion billeted for the night. The next day, the march continued to Watten, where it again billeted for the night. The Battalion left Watten at 10.15am the following morning, marching to Mentque in the Nordausques training area, where the four Companies split into three billets: 'A' Company at La Ronville, 'B' and 'C' Companies at Mentque, 'D' Company at Inglingham. The 27th was spent drill training, and the 28th was musketry training on a 400-yard range, followed by recreational training in the afternoon: football.

Battalion casualties for February 1917 were 3 killed and 4 wounded, all other ranks.[148] However, searching through the records, I found that there are six 8/KOYLI soldiers that died in February 1917, with just one actually killed in

[148] *8/KOYLI War Diary.*

action: Private 35410 Albert Denis Turner of Pontefract, on 6 February.[149] One other is simply recorded as having died on 16 February: Private 35349 Allen Oldroyd of Dewsbury.[150] Of the others, four died of wounds and the other died at home: Private 38349 John James Breckenridge of Castle Douglas, DoW, 15 February;[151] Private 29329 John James Brown of Newcastle, DaH, 15 February;[152] Private 13234 George Chappell of Leeds, DoW, 8 February;[153] Private 35417 Harry Walker of Sheffield, DoW, 8 February.[154]

March began with a new Battalion CO: Lieutenant-Colonel D. Quirk D.S.O., who took command on the 1st, having moved from 8/Y&LR. The Battalion resumed musketry training, followed by recreational training; probably a football re-match. The following day, 75 men arrived from Divisional Training Camp to join the Battalion, all other ranks. Further training continued over the next three days, which included *practising the attack* on 5 March. It was noted in the War Diary on the 8th that the officer who was on close and then open arrest, 2nd Lt J Riley, was facing a General Court-Martial (GCM) at Battalion HQ.

The rest of March was spent undertaking training in various aspects of soldiering and recreational training, which was very competitive; HQ won the football competition. The only exception was a march to Moulle on the 19th, to Bollezeele on the 20th and then to billets at Houtkerque on the 21st. The 22nd was spent resting, and training resumed on the 23rd, continuing into April. The only casualty for March was 1 soldier having died, not killed or died of his wounds, so I assume of some sickness or disease, an accident, or his death simply

---

149 Private 35410 Albert Denis Turner, aged 19, son of Denis and Bertha Turner of 38 Newgate, Pontefract. Buried at Railway Dugouts Burial Ground (Transport Farm), Grave number VII.G.15.

150 Private 35349 Allen Oldroyd, aged 32, husband of Florence Oldroyd of Pit Yard, Scouts Hill, Dewsbury. Buried at Boulogne Eastern Cemetery, Grave number VIII.B.187.

151 Private 38349 John James Breckenridge, aged 32, son of William and Agnes Breckenridge of Crossmichael, Kirkudbrightshire. Buried at Wimereux Communal Cemetery, Grave number II.D.11. Formerly with KOSB.

152 There is no CWGC record of Private 29329 John James Brown. This is likely because he died at home.

153 Private 13234 George Chappell, aged 21, son of Ada Chappell of 14 Victoria Grove, York Road, Leeds. Buried at Wimereux Communal Cemetery, Grave number II.D.1A.

154 Private 35417 Harry Walker, aged 31, husband of Julia Walker of 22/2 Matilda Street, Sheffield. Buried at Lijssenthoek Military Cemetery, Grave number XI.A.7.

not recorded properly. This was Private 34353 John Henry Mills of Wakefield, who died on 21 March.[155]

It was also noted that 2nd Lieutenant J Riley was dismissed from service at the GMC; still, no indication as to what for. For George, March 1917 was a memorable month, for it was on 17 March that he was promoted to Acting Sergeant. Achieving promotion in the field tells us that George had regularly gone above and beyond expectations, for this was the only route to a battlefield promotion.

Training at Houtkerque continued until 5 April, when the Battalion marched to Winnipeg Camp near Ourderdom, where training continued for another two days before another march to support positions in front of Ypres, where it relieved 1/20th London Regiment on 8 April. Battalion HQ and 'D' Company took up positions in railway dugouts, and the other three Companies at Zillebeke Bund. It is here on the next day, that the Front Line and a light railway in Hill 60[156] sub-sector came under heavy enemy bombardment, increasing in intensity from 6.00pm, when the shelling spread to the rear and continued until dusk; two soldiers were wounded.

On 10 April, 'C' Company relieved a company of the 11th Sherwood Foresters at a farmhouse that the British had christened 'Battersea' Farm. The next day, 'A' and 'D' Companies went into the Front Line, 'B' Company in support, and 'C' Company in reserve. Battalion HQ moved to Rudkin House. One man was wounded on 11 April.

The Battalion spent the next three days in the trenches and, on being relieved by the 8th Battalion East Yorkshire Regiment, went to rest at Busseboom. Three officers and two other ranks were wounded on 14 April. On 19 April, 'B', 'C' and 'D' Companies went to the railway dugouts for working parties and 'A' Company did further training. The Battalion went back into the Front Line on the 22nd, relieving the 10th Battalion West Riding Regiment on the right of the Brigade Front: 'B' and 'C' Companies in the line, 'D' Company in support and 'A' Company in reserve. Just one other rank was wounded on the 22nd.

---

[155] Private 34353 John Henry Mills, aged 39, husband of Mrs Binns (formerly Mills) of 37 Milton Street, Westgate, Wakefield. Buried at Lijssenthoek Military Cemetery, Grave number XI.C.9.

[156] Hill 60 is an area of raised land separated by the railway line to Comines, located 2.9 miles from the centre of Ypres. Before the Great War it was known locally as Côte des Amants (Lover's Knoll). It is now a battlefield memorial site and park.

Casualties increased on the 23rd, with five wounded and one suffering shell-shock; all were other ranks. There were seven wounded on the next day, and another died of wounds. Although no name is recorded in the War Diary, records show that this was 'D' Company Private 13386 Tom Ayres from Sheffield.[157] The 25th saw two other ranks killed and four wounded. Again, no names of those killed were recorded in the War Diary, but records show that they were Private 35559 John Ellis[158] from Sheffield and Private 27319 Percy Sendall[159] from Leeds.

On 26 April, the Battalion was relieved from the line by 9/Y&LR and went into support at the railway dugouts. The next three days were spent on working parties, and on the 30th, the Battalion went back in the line at Hill 60 sub-sector, relieving 11/SF; 'A' and 'D' Companies in the line, 'B' Company in support and 'C' Company in reserve. One other rank was recorded wounded on the 29th.

As 8/KOYLI continued to defend the trenches during the prelude to the British offensive that would be known as the Battle of Messines (7–14 June 1917), the Battalion would be missing Acting Sergeant George Harry Pridmore, for on 15 April he had returned to England as he had been formally recommended as a suitable candidate for a temporary commission by 8/KOYLI Commanding Officer, Lieutenant-Colonel D. Quirk, on 31 March 1917; yet another battlefield promotion for George. Whilst no doubt George had earned this opportunity, the casualty rate of subalterns was so high by this time that the Army was desperate to increase their numbers and, having used up much of the 'gentleman' sources, had to increasingly raise them from the ranks. The 1914 subaltern intake had come mainly from the public school-educated 'upper' class; men of superior quality and 'born to lead':

---

157 Private Tom Ayres, aged 25, son of John Thomas Ayres of Sheffield, husband of Theresa Marshal (formerly Ayres) of 8/2 St John's Road, Park, Sheffield. Buried at Railway Dugouts Burial Ground (Transport Farm), Grave number VII.G.32.

158 Private John Ellis, aged 19, son of John and Ruth Ellis of 26 Court, 4 House, Saville Street East, Sheffield. Buried at Railway Dugouts Burial Ground (Transport Farm), Grave number VII.E.24.

159 Private Percy Sendall, aged 25, son of the late William and Ann Ellen Sendall of Leeds. Buried at Railway Dugouts Burial Ground (Transport Farm), Grave number VII.E.25.

'The soldier in his hour of need and danger will ever be more ready to follow an officer and gentleman whom education, position in life, and accident of birth point out to be his natural leader ... than the man who, by dint of study and brain work, has raised himself (much to his own credit, certainly) from the plough or anvil.'[160]

On his return to England, George first reported to the KOYLI Regimental Depot at Pontefract, where he was formally accepted as a candidate on 5 July 1917 and posted to join one of the Officer Training Battalions at Gailes Camp in Scotland. Whilst back in England, and before going to Scotland, he would learn that his brother, Albert, had been wounded on 2 May and was at Bradford Hospital. I hope that he was granted compassionate leave and was able to see him before he passed away on 22 June. The loss of a third brother would have hit George hard and dampened the euphoria for his imminent prospects, for not only was he looking forward to a commission, but he had also planned to get married whilst he was in England. Although he didn't need permission to get married, he would have notified his CO of his intention to marry. It is not known how long he had known his future wife, 22-year-old May Foster, but I guess it would have been long before being posted to Belgium that they had met. Being posted back to England for his officer training offered them an opportunity to marry, which they did on 2 September 1917 at St Mary's Church, Walkley, in Sheffield; no doubt a joyous occasion, but with melancholic thoughts of his absent brothers.

Passing-out group of newly commissioned officers at Gailes Camp, August 1917
(*https://www.greatwarforum.org/*)

[160] Hamilton, Lieutenant-General Sir Frederick, from *Origins and History of the First or Grenadier Guards,* 1874, quoted in op. cit. Lewis-Sempell, pp.13–14.

Gailes Camp was established in March 1916, when it was occupied by the Royal Scots Fusiliers. The 9th and 10th Officer Training Battalions (OTB) were based at the camp, and each trained 400 officers at a time, increasing to 600 after 1917 responding to the urgent need for subalterns in the field. George joined the 9th OTB for training at Gailes, which was for a four-and–a-half-month course, but he was able to excuse himself during this period to get married. He also spent five days in the Gailes Camp hospital from 22 September to 26 September 1917. The reason for this admission on his medical record simply states: *'Headache (128)'*. The 128 must be significant and possibly a code number for a particular reason for the headache, perhaps delayed battlefield fatigue. He obviously recovered and was able to satisfactorily complete his training, for he was discharged from 8/KOYLI on 30 October 1917, having served for 3 years and 291 days. He then re-enlisted with his commission of temporary Second Lieutenant to the West Yorkshire Regiment (Prince of Wales Own); newly commissioned men could not return to their original regiment.

George became what was known to the troops as a *'one pip wonder'*,[161] one of about 229,000 new commissions that were granted during the War, 107,929 of which had passed through the Officer Training Corps (OTC) after serving in the ranks.[162] The other officers called them *'Temporary Gentlemen'*, or '*TGs'*.

On joining the West Yorkshire Regiment, George was assigned to the 21st Battalion (Wool Textile Pioneers).[163] The date of his return to France and Belgium is not clear. His commission was published in the *London Gazette* dated 23 November 1917, and another date on his records under the abbreviation "M.S.1 (K.)" is 8 December 1917. I have not been able to ascertain what the abbreviation stands for. However, on searching the 21/WYR War Diary, the earliest date that new officers joined the Battalion, and could include George, is 14 January 1918. I will use this as the date he was likely to have joined his new Regiment in the field.

---

[161] Op. cit. Holmes, p. 497.

[162] Ibid., p. 580.

[163] The 21st Battalion (Wool Textile Pioneers) was formed in Halifax on 24 September 1915 by the Lord Mayor of Leeds and moved to Skipton in February 1916. The Battalion moved to France in June 1916. The Wool Textile moniker probably derived from their Halifax connection. Pioneer Battalions were employed in engineering and construction work in the field but would invariably be used in the trenches when required.

It wasn't unusual for a newly commissioned officer to spend some time assimilating to his new Regiment, which would include some induction training. It is also possible that George had some leave whilst still in England, which would be welcome for the newly-wed. Nevertheless, it wouldn't be too long before he had to return to the War, and as a subaltern, he would have responsibility for at least a platoon of men.

On 14 and 15 January 1918, George's new Battalion, the 21/WYR, was in Tilloy-lès-Mofflaines in the Hauts-de-France region of France, 3 km south-east of Arras, undertaking maintenance of communication trenches and tramways, and the construction of strong points and machine gun nests at 'Happy Valley'.[164] Whilst men of Pioneer Battalions were predominantly employed on construction and engineering work, and generally not as exposed to combat conditions, and consequently relatively safer than regular infantrymen, they very often came under enemy artillery fire and, at times of necessity, were used to reinforce the Front Line as required, for they were also trained infantrymen. Depending on where they were working, such as Happy Valley above, which was an important strategic position, they would be regular targets for the German Artillery. The comparative casualty rates are reflected in the War Diary reports, from which the following narrative on the Battalion's movements and activities is derived.

On 16 January, 'A' Company was resting, whilst 'B', 'C' and 'D' Companies started work on a support line in one of the systems of trenches; 'A' Company joined the other three on this work on the following day. On the 18th, the digging of new trenches was abandoned, as all four Companies were deployed on reclaiming and revetting[165] trenches that had collapsed due to heavy rainfall. Communication trenches had become impassable, requiring overland board tracks to be laid. The reclaiming work continued until the 24th, when all Companies were detailed to work on the reserve line, with small parties working on a new support line behind the reserve line. This work continued for the rest of January.

---

[164] *Happy Valley* was the name given to the long valley which ran eastwards from Orange Hill, and along which Commonwealth troops fought their way on 10–11 April 1917, during the early stages of the Battle of Arras, which was now in British hands. Orange Hill is due north of Tilloy-les-Mofflaines. There are Great War cemeteries at both Happy Valley and Orange Hill.

[165] Revetting: to face a wall or embankment with stones.

During this period (14–31 January), the Battalion recorded casualties on just three days: 22nd, 2 other ranks wounded; 29th, 1 other rank wounded; 31st, 1 other rank killed: Private 21/929 George Henry Perrett.[166]

At the start of February, the fighting strength of 21/WYR was 37 officers and 757 other ranks. Work continued on reclaiming and revetting reserve trenches and repairing tramways. On 4 February, the Battalion was joined by 2 officers and 40 other ranks from the West Yorkshire Regiment's 18th Battalion, and 50 other ranks, who were formerly Royal Engineers men, left the Battalion and were drafted to Rouen. One other rank was wounded on this day.

On the following day, 'D' Company was relieved by the 9th Battalion Gordon Highlanders and moved to billets in Arras. The remainder of 21/WYR moved to Arras on 7 February. The next seven days were spent at Arras, where the Battalion undertook company training and recreation that included football and tug-of-war. On the 12th, advance parties were sent to St Laurent Blangy, and on the 13th the Battalion billets were inspected by the Acting GOC, Major Edwin Finn (Lt-Col Sir E.H. St L Clarke having been wounded in the leg on 10 October 1917), who also inspected the Battalion in marching order on the 15th before it moved off to join the advance parties at St Laurent Blangy. The next day, 'C' Company moved to Les Fosses Farm for work under Commanding Royal Engineers (CRE) of the 15th Division. One other rank wounded on this day (16 February).

On 17 February, 'A', 'B' and 'D' Companies spent the day digging and wiring reserve trenches on either side of the River Scarpe, while 'C' Company were wiring a trench known as Gordon Avenue; five other ranks were wounded. This work continued until 25 February, with work starting on two deep dug-outs on the 21st. One officer and three other ranks suffered from being gassed on the 19th, and three other ranks were wounded on the 25th. On the 26th, Major Finn inspected Battalion billets and transport, and 21/WYR was reorganised into three Companies: 'X', 'Y' and 'Z'. On the last day of February, 2nd Lt Mitchell joined the Battalion, bringing the strength up to 40 officers and 749 other ranks.

For the first ten days of March 1918, the Battalion's three Companies worked on reserve trenches for XVII Corps, with the exception of half of 'Y' Company, which was sent to XV (Scottish) Infantry Division for the duration, returning on

[166] Private George Henry Perrett, son of Thomas Nichols Perrett (York Station Master) of Bell Busk, Craven District of North Yorkshire, husband of Emma Perrett. Buried at Monchy British Cemetery, Monchy-le-Preux, Grave number II.B.28.

11 March. During these 11 days, two men were wounded on the 6th, and 50 other ranks joined the Battalion on the 9th. On 11 March, the Battalion moved to billets in Arras, resting on the 12th, when a further 50 other ranks joined them. On the 13th, all three Companies returned to work on the XVII Corps reserve trenches until 21 March. Another 26 other ranks joined the Battalion on the 17th, and two men were wounded on the 21st. The 21st was also the day that Lt-Col Clarke returned to take command of the Battalion, having recovered from his injuries.

On 22 March, the Battalion marched to Rifle Camp, and another man was wounded. At dawn the following day, the three Companies were assigned to three separate Brigades to occupy their respective reserve trenches. Then late orders were received for the Battalion to move back to Duisans, 5 miles north-west of Arras. By the time all Companies were reassembled and able to leave camp, it was 10.00pm, arriving at Duisans at 1.00am on the morning of the 24th. During the 23rd, Major Finn was severely wounded, and four other ranks were wounded. The Battalion worked on the Army lines from 9.00am until 5.00pm, returning the following day to continue the work until orders were received later to march back to Rifle Camp, arriving there at midnight. Nine other ranks joined the Battalion on the 25th. At dawn on 26 March, the three Companies were sent into the reserve trenches, which they spent the day improving. Continuing this work on the following day, they came under heavy German shellfire and suffered heavy casualties: 16 killed (all Privates) and 42 wounded – the Battalion's heaviest loss in a single day. See Appendix 3 for details of those killed.

Eight more men were killed on the following day, 28 March, with 40 more wounded; 2 officers and 1 other rank were also gassed. 21/WYR was now attached to the 10th Brigade and was holding the line south of the River Scarpe. The Battalion moved forward at 6.30pm in conjunction with two Companies of the Duke of Wellington Regiment and a Battalion of the King's Own Scottish Borderers of the 15th Division and dug in about 1,000 yards in front of the line and held this position. In addition to the 8 men killed, two more died of their wounds this day, probably from the previous day's bombardment. See Appendix 4 for details of all ten who died on the 28th.

The 29th was spent improving trenches and positions until being relieved by the 14th Battalion Royal Warwickshire Regiment during the night, reassembling at Rifle Camp at 4.00am on the 30th. The War Diary records casualties as being

2 other ranks wounded, but in the history of the Regiment,[167] one Private 4/8241 Walker Bedford[168] is recorded as DoW on 28 March 1918 and recorded at CWGC as died on 29 March 1918.

In the afternoon of 30 March, the Battalion marched to dugouts at St Laurent-Blangy, and from this base, began work on the support line trenches to the north of the Arras-Fampoux road. This work continued on the next day; Regimental Sergeant Major Gibbs and one other rank were wounded. At the end of March, the fighting strength of 21/WYR was 25 officers and 551 other ranks.

On 1 April, 'Y' Company was delegated to work with the 12th Brigade, whilst 'X' and 'Z' Companies continued to work on the support trenches; one man was wounded. This situation continued for the next week, with work continuing at various points on the support trenches and under both 11th and 12th Brigades, as well as 10th Brigade. On 5 April, Lieutenant F. Richardson and three other ranks of 'Z' Company were wounded. On 6 April, 'X' Company lost one man killed and two wounded. The man killed was Private 14325 Harold Randell.[169] That there is no grave for Harold Randell suggests that his body was not recovered. One man died of his wounds on 5 April – Private 53257 Charles Cramp[170] – who may well have been the man wounded on 1 April. Another man died of his wounds on 7 April – Private 238108 William Goodall Watson[171] – and perhaps one of the casualties of the 6th.

Over the 7th and 8th of April, the Battalion was relieved by the 1st Canadian Pioneers and entrained for Fosseux, where the men went into rest, their only work was to clean up the huts that they were given. On the 9th and 10th of April, the Battalion received reinforcements numbering 10 officers and 199 other ranks

---

[167] Wyrall, Everard, *The West Yorkshire Regiment in the War 1914–1918, Volume Two*, The Naval & Military Press, p. 487.

[168] Private 4/8241 Walker Bedford, ward of Mrs Pyrah of 17 Annie Street, Morley, Leeds, buried at Duisans British Cemetery, Etrun, Grave number V.F.44.

[169] Private 14325 Harold Randell, grandson of Mary Ann Randell of 113 Osler Street, Ladywood, Birmingham, commemorated at Arras Memorial, Bay 4.

[170] Private 53257 Charles Cramp, aged 19, son of Mr & Mrs George Cramp of Ring Fence, Shepshed, Leicestershire, buried at Athies Communal Cemetery Extension, Grave number M.11.

[171] Private 238108 William Goodall Watson, aged 21, son of Henry and Elizabeth Watson of 'The Wheat Sheaf', New Road, Gravesend, buried at Duisans British Cemetery, Etrun, Grave number VI.F.60.

on the 9th and 33 other ranks on the 10th. The new members, described in the War Diary as *'good lads, just under 19'*, had a few days being allocated to their respective Companies and getting to know their new comrades before the Battalion marched off at 10.30am on 12 April to a transport point on the Arras-Doullens road to await buses to a point between Lillers and Busnes, where they bivouacked in fields for the night. The diarist remarked that they were kept waiting from 12.00 to 4.00pm for their buses.

British troops and their buses at Arras (Imperial War Museum)

The following day (13 April), they set off on the march once more to billets in Le Cornet Bourdois. The next day, the Battalion moved to a camp and billets at the Château de Werppe. All three companies were put to work that night in trenches at Les Harisoirs, a line that followed the road that was a regular target for German Artillery; work such as this, undertaken in no-man's land or close to the German trenches, was often undertaken at night under cover of darkness. Lieutenant Bulmer and 13 men of 'X' Company were wounded.

Seventeen more men were drafted into the Battalion on 15 April, and the night work continued into the following day, when one 'Y' Company man was wounded. On the 17th, all three Companies were engaged in digging new trenches between Hinges and the Canal d'Aire; one more man wounded. On the 18th, 'X' and 'Y' Companies continued with the digging of the new trenches, while 'Z' Company started digging another new trench near Les Harisoirs. Casualties mounted up this day, with Lieutenant Bertram Cecil Metcalfe-

Smith[172] being wounded and dying later in the day, four other 'Z' Company ranks were wounded. Three men of 'Y' Company were killed on their way to the trenches they were digging, and nine were wounded, all casualties of shellfire. The three soldiers killed were Private 18/133 Ephraim Marshall Harrison;[173] Private 40228 Albert Jagger[174] and Private 52458 George Mellor.[175] They were buried in consecutive graves at Gonnehem British Cemetery. Also noted in the War Diary on this day was that a strong attack by the enemy on the 4th Division's front was completely beaten off, with about 160 German prisoners taken.

The digging of new trenches continued the following day (19 April), and six more men were wounded. Heavy German shelling continued into 20 April, and three platoons of 'X' Company had to return to base, as they were simply unable to work for the barrage. Second Lieutenant James Burness Grange[176] was killed, along with one other rank, and eight more were wounded; all of 'X' Company. The other man killed was Private 58278 Tom Richards.[177]

It is here that we leave 21/WYR for a while, as George Harry was transferred to the 2nd Battalion Essex Regiment on 21 April, along with 2nd Lt J Camplin; 2/Essex was short of subalterns, having lost so many on the Front Line. It is

---

[172] Lieutenant Bertram Cecil Metcalfe-Smith of 4th Battalion, West Yorkshire Regiment, was on secondment to 21/WYR, aged 24, son of Reginald and Kate Frances Metcalfe-Smith of Nunirons, Olney, Buckinghamshire, buried at Pernes British Cemetery, Grave number I.D.13

[173] Private 18/133 Ephraim Marshall Harrison, aged 26, son of William and Dinah Harrison of Bradford, buried at Gonnehem British Cemetery, Grave number A.12

[174] Private 40228 Albert Jagger, aged 40, son of Alice Jagger of 13 Albion Street, Queensbury, Bradford, buried at Gonnehem British Cemetery, Grave number A.10

[175] Private 52458 George Mellor, aged 18, son of Harriet Mellor and the late Henry Mellor of Sturston Road, Ashbourne, Derbyshire, buried at Gonnehem British Cemetery, Grave number A.11

[176] Second Lieutenant James Burness Grange, aged 27, son of William D'Oyly Grange MD (late Surgeon Major, 3rd Battalion King's Own Scottish Borderers) and Mrs Grange (neé Burness) of 3 Clarence Drive, Harrogate. Born at Moffat, Dumfriesshire. Bachelor of Science (BSA) of University of Toronto, Canada, and Assistant Inspector, Board of Agriculture, England. Buried at Gonnehem British Cemetery, Grave number A.19

[177] Private 58278 Tom Richards, formerly 194175 Royal Field Artillery (RFA), aged 39, son of Thomas and Mary Ann Richards of Cardiff, buried at Gonnehen British Cemetery, Grave number A.20

ironic that 2nd Lt Grange had also volunteered to transfer, but he was on another journey.

Arriving for duty with 2/Essex on 22 April, George and his fellow 21/WYR officer colleague were welcomed with a baptism of fire. Whilst George had experienced Front Line fighting with 8/KOYLI as a Private, his time with the Pioneers had statistically reduced the likelihood of becoming a casualty, even though his commission made him more vulnerable to a sniper's bullet. Certainly, he was used to artillery fire and death amongst the ranks whilst out in the field, and he may have also been a member of one of the 21/WYR Companies to have been sent to reinforce the Front Line and had experienced it first-hand as an officer. Whatever he expected on volunteering to join 2/Essex, I doubt that the fighting that he had been involved in was as intense as that which he was about to experience.

On the day that they arrived, the two West Yorkshire men were assigned to 'B' and 'C' Companies, which were filling a gap in the Line between the 61st Division and Lancashire Fusiliers. The next day, 2nd Lt Camplin was wounded, and George received a slight wound that required him to attend *'FA'*, which I interpret as Field Ambulance, or, in other words, the Regimental Aid Post (RAP). One other officer – 2nd Lt J L. Elliston – was also wounded. Before George was able to return to duty, the Battalion had been relieved and had moved to billets at Cense-la-Valles; the casualties list was certainly something George wasn't ready for. From 16 April to 24 April inclusive, 2/Essex had lost 43 other ranks killed; 115 wounded; 36 missing; 42 sent to RAP; and 2 died of wounds. Also on the 24th, 2nd Lt Wilfred Herbert Nunneley[178] went missing, and Captain J Tomlinson was wounded. Second Lieutenant Nunneley is recorded as being killed between 23 and 24 April 1918. Two Lieutenants and thirteen 2nd Lieutenants joined 2/Essex on 24 April.

The next three days were spent reorganising the Battalion, cleaning up the wounded and transporting those who needed further treatment to the CCS. On 28 April, the Battalion went back into the Front Line, relieving 1st Battalion Somerset Light Infantry: 'A' and 'B' Companies in the line at Pacaut Wood, with 'C' and 'D' Companies in support on the Canal bank. Three other ranks were sent to RAP, and seven more officers joined the Battalion on this day.

---

[178] Second Lieutenant Wilfred Herbert Nunneley, aged 19, son of Arthur and Emma Nunneley of Waterloo House, 146 High Street, St Barnet, Herts, commemorated at Loos Memorial, Panel 85 to 87.

The Battalion maintained its position on the 29th, but with further casualties. Second Lieutenant Frederick Corn[179] and 2nd Lt Noel Bertram Barrett[180] had been two of the subalterns to join 2/Essex on the 24th, and both were killed on the 29th, along with one other rank. Four other ranks were wounded, and one more sent to RAP. The last day of April was spent once more in the line with more casualties: 9 other ranks were wounded, and 7 were sent to RAP.

The Battalion was relieved by the 2nd Battalion Lancashire Fusiliers on 1 May and went into reserve at Bellerive with Battalion HQ; nine other ranks were wounded and four more sent to RAP. Five more officers joined the Battalion on the 2nd, but it lost one more other rank killed and four more were wounded. The next day, 3 May, Battalion HQ had to vacate the farm that they had set themselves up in due to fire and moved to Mt Bernenchon. One more other rank was wounded, and six others sent to RAP. Ten others were despatched to CCS.

It was back to the Front Line for the Battalion on 4 May. Having relieved 1/KOSB, 'C' and 'D' Companies went into the line, 'A' Company in support at Pacaut Wood, and 'B' Company in reserve along the Canal bank. Four more casualties by way of two other ranks wounded and four sent to RAP. 2/Essex maintained its position with 'C' Company advancing its line in what is described as *'peaceful penetration'* until being relieved by 2nd Battalion Seaforth Highlanders on 7 May, moving to billets at Busnettes; two other ranks were wounded and seven more to CCS.

The next two days were spent reorganising the Battalion and sorting wounded, with two more going to CCS and two to RAP; eighteen more reinforcements arrived on 8 May.

As reorganising continued on the 9th, the diarist comments that the Battalion is *'feeling the need of good NCOs',* suggesting that a good number of the casualties had been NCOs, which hadn't been replaced by the reinforcements. Orders to 'stand to' were received as an enemy attack was expected in the early hours of either the 10th or 11th. The suspected intention was for the Germans to cross over the Canal under cover of darkness. The Battalion moved to 'stand to' positions around Mont-Bernenchon, but the all clear came at 4.30am on the 10th,

---

179 Second Lieutenant Frederick Corn, aged 27, son of John and Alice Corn of 68 Larch Road, Cricklewood, London, buried at Gonnehem British Cemetery, Grave number B.22

180 Second Lieutenant Noel Bertram Barrett, aged 19, son of Ernest James and Ada Frances Barrett of Yew Cottage, Kingston Road, Staines, buried at Gonnehen British Cemetery, Grave number B.20

and the men returned to billets at Busnettes, where they slept all day. That evening, the 'stand to' order came again, and the Battalion returned to trenches around Mont-Bernenchon. Ten more Battalion reinforcements arrived, but nine other ranks were sent to CCS, and two more to RAP.

Over the next four days, 2/Essex remained in the Front Line, with 'A' Company in the line, 'B' Company in support, and 'C' and 'D' Companies in reserve. There being no attacks or raids, only shelling, these days were recorded as being *'quiet'*. Nevertheless, 14 other ranks were sent to RAP, 11 to CCS, and 3 others and 1 officer were wounded; I am not sure why there are different records for what, in all intents and purposes, are wounded men. RAP and CCS are destinations of the wounded men, but where did those recorded as *'wounded'* go? I have been unable to find an explanation for these differences.

When we last left George, he was on his way to the RAP, and there is no record in the War Diary of when he returned to the Battalion. He may have been back within a day or a week, or he may have missed all of the above action and was still at RAP on 15 May, or he may even have been sent on to CCS. However, he may well have been back before this point, so I will continue the story assuming he is involved in one of the four Companies, probably leading a platoon. As we shall see, he does come back at some point.

The next five days are all recorded as *'quiet'* or *'very quiet'*. 2/SH relieved 'C' and 'D' Companies on 20 May, and 'A' and 'B' Companies remained on the Canal bank under the command of the 10th Infantry Brigade. Casualties between 16 and 20 May inclusive were 4 other ranks and 1 officer wounded; 15 sent to RAP; 16 sent to CCS and 1 other rank killed. Two more other ranks were '*struck off strength*', which I take to mean gone sick.

Back in Busnettes billets, the 21 May is spent cleaning up casualties, and on 22 May, training from the Armourer and Gas Specialist and wiring classes were the order of the day for 'C' and 'D' Companies, who later relieved 'A' and 'B' Companies on the Canal bank. For the first time, baths are mentioned – no doubt much welcomed – and inspections – probably not so much welcomed. The procedures at bath times would include the men's clothes being washed and de-loused. Lice were a constant problem in the trenches. On 24 May, the whole Battalion returned to the Front Line: 'B' Company in the line at Pacaut Wood, 'A' and 'C' Companies in support and 'D' Company in reserve on Canal bank. Once in position, the rest of the day is spent digging and improving the line and wiring.

The 25th was another quiet day, but at night, a patrol reported having killed a German sniper and found that he was using an English rifle and wearing an old civilian coat. It is here that we find that George Harry was on duty, as once more he was wounded and taken off to RAP along with two other 2nd Lieutenants and one other rank; one other rank was killed. The War Diary doesn't say whether George was one of the patrol members, but if he was, he would have led it, as officers always led platoons and patrols, unlike the Germans, whose patrols were led by NCOs, as were those of the Canadian Regiments.[181]

The trench digging and wiring were continued with haste the following day, and on the 27th, the men on the Canal bank came under some German Artillery fire due to a Special Company of Royal Engineers (RE) undertaking some *'elaborate preparations'* for firing gas bombs from this position. During the night, the RE used red and green rockets when the gas was due to be discharged. This highlighted their position to the German observers, and their artillery responded with H.E. and Shrapnel. 'C' Company relieved 'B' Company in the line, which then went into support.

On the 28th, 'D' Company HQ came under shellfire that became too close for comfort, so it vacated the house and moved to a shelter in the Canal bank. The British Artillery shelled the German back areas and the enemy second line during the night of the 29th, from midnight to 3.00am. 2/Essex continued with trench digging and wiring but found things difficult due to there being a full moon. The Canal bank came under even heavier enemy shellfire, with both H.E. and gas, on 31 May, but work continued, and the trench that they had been digging was now a continuous line, though shallow in places.

The Battalion's positions remained unchanged, and the casualty tally since 21 May was recorded as 35 other ranks and 3 officers (including 2nd Lt George Harry Pridmore) sent to RAP; 24 other ranks to CCS; 10 other ranks and 1 officer wounded and 3 other ranks killed.

The first of June was a quiet day, but the line received enemy gas during the night, with a number of 2/Essex casualties. The Battalion was relieved by 2/SH on the 2nd, and it went into reserve back at Busnettes. The following day was spent clearing casualties, and the rest of the week consisted of training, building a rifle range, and Company by Company partaking of baths and disinfection. Further gas attacks brought more casualties, and there was a dribble of

---

[181] Op. cit. Lewis-Stempel, p. 111.

reinforcements. Once the rifle range was finished, further training ensued, including attacking formation.

On 8 June, the Battalion moved back into the line at 8.30pm, relieving 1/Somerset Light Infantry: 'D' Company in the line; 'B' Company in close support; 'A' Company in reserve and 'C' Company on the Canal bank. Battalion HQ was now at Pompadour Farm.

The next day, work was allocated on digging a new communications trench from the support line to the Front. This work continued for the next ten days, with Companies exchanging positions at various times. An anticipated attack by the Germans on the 11th didn't materialise, but casualties were recorded every day from shelling and gas attacks, including one other rank being killed on 17 June following a Divisional advance on the Battalion's right, under a barrage of British Artillery, which brought some retaliation from the Germans. The communications trench was completed on the 18th, but *'the parapet and parados were not good.'*

The 19th was a quiet day, with just the support line gaining the attention of German shelling. During the night of 19/20 June, the Battalion was relieved by 2/SH and returned to billets at Busnettes, where a strange disease had been classified by the *'Medical Authorities',* they had labelled it *'4 Day Fever'.* This would account for the number of men struck of strength; 72 cases had been admitted to hospital during the Battalion's last tour.

Back at Busnettes, clearing up and reorganisation were the order of the day. The next day, 'A' and 'B' Companies went to the baths and 'C' Company to the rifle range for *'specialist training.'* The 23rd was a Sunday, and a Church Parade was undertaken in a field by Battalion HQ. Church Parade wasn't optional in the British Army, and all had to attend, whatever their religious leanings, a tradition dating back to the English Civil War. They didn't occur every Sunday, as a Chaplain may not always be available, but wherever he was, he would be facilitating the service somewhere behind the lines.

In the afternoon, there was a football match, and a performance of the 4th Division Follies followed in the evening. Despite a recreational day, there were 17 casualties.

A Church Parade in the field early in the War

On Monday, 24 June, it was 'B' Company's turn for specialist training on the rifle range. The rest of the Battalion trained in a practise attack by Company formation. There must still have been some gas around, as despite the Battalion being on training exercises, there were still 49 casualties, although 24 were *'evacuated'*, which may infer the 4 Day Fever. Later on in the day, the Battalion went back into the line, relieving 1/Somerset. The line was pretty quiet, and the pattern of the Battalion's previous time in the line was much the same this time around. The diarist reported a successful raid by 1/Warwicks on the left of 2/Essex on the 30 June, capturing three German prisoners and suffering no casualties.

Over the next week, the Battalion remained in the line, but it was quiet, allowing time for position improvements and for sending patrols out to see what the Germans were up to. Fresh reinforcements arrived to increase strength, but further casualties depleted strength as more wounded men were sent to the RAP. Two men were killed on 5 July, one being 2nd Lt William Walter Nash, who was on secondment from 3/Essex,[182] and the other being one of the other ranks. The 2nd Lancashire Fusiliers made a successful raid on the night of 6 July, which

[182] Second Lieutenant William Walter Nash, aged 28, son of the late Walter Nash of Hornsey, London, husband of Bertha Eugen Nash of 72 Cecile Park, Crouch End, London, buried at Mont-Bernanchon British Cemetery, Gonnehem, Grave number I.J.8

prompted some retaliatory shelling from the German Artillery; three men were wounded. The shelling increased during the next day, and the Battalion HQ received a direct hit; two other ranks were wounded. The Battalion was relieved by 1/SH and returned to billets at Busnettes.

The 8 July was spent cleaning up and with inspections; one more other rank was killed. Two Companies spent the 9th at baths and disinfection, and their clothes and boots were repaired. One Company was practicing at the rifle range. Thirty-three reinforcements arrived, and 4 other ranks went to RAP. The process was repeated the next day with different Companies at the baths, and classes for Lewis Gunners were held in the field. One Company attended the rifle range on the 11th, and specialist training was carried out under the 'Specialist Officer' and NCOs. The practice of attack by platoons was also undertaken. Six men joined the Battalion, and 7 men went to RAP. Intermittent training carried on until 13 July, when the Battalion relieved the 1st Somerset Light Infantry in the Front Line, with 'D' Company in the line, 'A' Company in support and 'C' and 'B' Companies in reserve. Battalion HQ was at Pompadour Farm, and the situation remained very quiet all day on 14 July.

Recent heavy rain had impacted the trenches, and Companies set to work repairing them without interference from the enemy, who remained very quiet again on the 15th. The comings and goings of a number of officers and the exchange of Companies in the line were the highlights of the War Diary for the rest of the week, and on 18 July, the War Diary records 2nd Lt G.R. Pridmore and 2nd Lt W.L. Knight joining the Battalion for duty. This has to be George Harry, and the 'R' should have been 'H'. I can find no other record of a G.R. Pridmore anywhere, let alone in 2/Essex. This has to be George returning from his injuries of 25 May, which, if I am right, were more substantial than 'slight'.

From 19–23 July, the Battalion remained in the line with very little enemy activity to trouble the men. Companies exchanged line positions again on the 23rd. German activity increased during the early hours of the morning of the 24th and continued at intervals during the day. On the following day, 'A' Company raided German trenches, only to find them empty, and they returned with no casualties. The German Artillery opened up but did no significant damage. It was a day of change for George, though. There had been a number of subaltern reinforcements this week, and it was on 25 July that George returned to his old Battalion: 21/WYR. So we leave the 2/Essex in the trenches, with little enemy activity, and focus once more on the 2nd Battalion West Yorkshire Regiment at La Vallée.

It is worth considering at this point just how vulnerable George Harry was as a subaltern. He had been wounded twice whilst with the 2/Essex, but we don't know what George was doing at the time that he was wounded or what the nature of his wounds was. His duties as a Second Lieutenant would include responsibilities for at least a platoon of men, and he would lead them into any offensive action. The term *'over the top'* comes to mind when we think of the British Tommy attacking the Hun. And before a change in the Army Manual in 1917,[183] officers were the first out of the trench to attack the Germans, often a futile rush into a hail of machine-gun bullets that mowed the infantrymen down like a scythe through corn. The officer was the first and principal target, and he was easily identified with his uniform and with being armed with a pistol, not a rifle, although many officers realised this and took to wearing a Private's uniform and to carrying a rifle. But he was still the first target to appear for German machine-gunners and snipers. The average life expectancy of a British junior officer during the worst phase of the War on the Western Front was just six weeks.[184]

Their vulnerability, compared to other ranks, was borne out by the statistics:

	Officers killed	Other ranks killed
1 October 1914 – 30 September 1915	14.2%	5.8%
1 October 1915 – 30 September 1916	8.0%	4.9%
1 October 1916 – 30 September 1917	8.5%	4.7%
1 October 1917 – 30 September 1918	6.9%	4.0%

A similar differential arises when comparing officers and other ranks wounded: between 1 October 1914 and 30 September 1915, 24.4% of officers were wounded compared to 17.4% of other ranks.[185] The Second Lieutenant, or subaltern, was the most dangerous rank in the whole British Army on the

[183] New Army Manual: SS143, *Instructions for the Training of Platoons for Offensive Action.* See op. cit. Lewis-Stempel, p. 215.

[184] Ibid., p. 5.

[185] Ibid., p. 183.

Western Front. Of all of those who served on the Western Front during the course of the Great War, 12% were killed or died of wounds.[186]

There was no record entered in the 21/WYR War Diary of George's return to the Battalion, which was busy refitting and converting trenches in the support line of the British Front at La Vallée, where it had been since the end of April. A platoon of 'Z' Company was also laying a mile-long tramway to the support line. The fighting strength of 21/WYR at the end of July was 26 officers and 566 other ranks.

The beginning of August found 21/WYR 'X' and 'Y' Companies converting a trench known as *'Cream Trench'* to breastwork and parados, and continuing revetment of another trench called *'Battle Trench'*. 'Z' Company was constructing posts in a trench named *'Peacock Trench'*. Four men of 'X' Company were wounded on 1 August. This work continued for the next seven days, only interrupted by heavy rain on 2 August. On the 8th, all Companies were employed on repairing and clearing roads towards Paradis, behind the advancing British Army; one 'Y' Company man was wounded. This work continued up until 23 August as the British advance continued, with just 'Y' Company taking a day out for training on the 14th. On the 24th, having finished their stint on the roads, the Battalion marched from La Vallée to Camblain Château, where they entrained for Framecourt on the 25th.

From Framecourt, the Battalion marched to Camblain l'abbé the next day, where they spent time resting on the 27th. On 28 August, 21/WYR moved by bus back into the line at Fosse Farm, east of Monchy. The next day, work began clearing and repairing roads to the continually moving Front Line, with Germans in retreat; the War was once more a mobile war, leaving the stalemate of the trenches behind. There were more casualties, with two 'X' Company men being wounded and Sergeant 21/244 W.H. Moxon[187] being killed. Continuing with the road work, two more 'X' Company men were wounded the following day, 30 August.

The last day of August 1918 was the last day of the life 22-year-old Second Lieutenant George Harry Pridmore. There is no indication of how George was killed in the War Diary, just a simple *'killed'*. Four other ranks were wounded that day. The Battalion was working on the roads, and George is recorded in de

---

186 Ibid., p. 25.

187 Sergeant 21/244 W.H. Moxon is buried at Feuchy Chapel British Cemetery, Wancourt, Grave number I.G.8

Ruvigny's as being killed in action on the Cambrai Road. The Battalion was not actually engaged in battle with the enemy, so we may assume that he died as a result of shellfire. The alternative would be a sniper's bullet, sniper's often stalked alone to identify British officer targets. Or maybe a German raiding party, but this is unlikely, with them being in retreat. As with John, Arthur and Albert, we shall never know the exact circumstances of George's death, but I hope it was instant.

George is buried at Feuchy Chapel British Cemetery, Wancourt, Grave number I.F.10. The personal inscription on his headstone reads 'BEAUTIFUL MEMORIES SHADOWED BY GRIEF'.

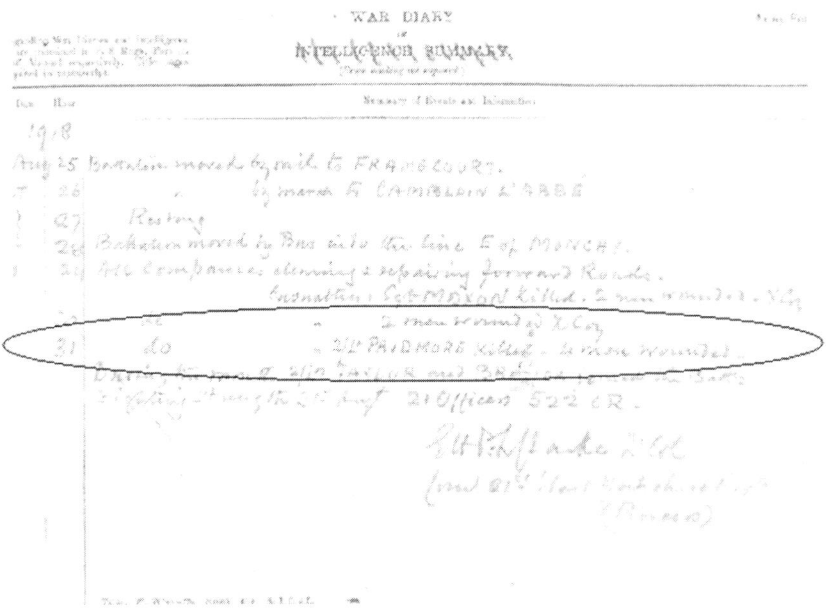
WAR DIARY
or
INTELLIGENCE SUMMARY.

1918

Aug 25 Battalion moved by rail to FRANSCOURT.
26 " by march to CAMBLAIN L'ABBE
27 Resting
28 Battalion moved by Bus into the line E of MONCHY.
29 All Companies cleaning & repairing forward Roads.
Casualties: Sgt MOXON killed. 2 men wounded.
30 do " 2 men wounded X Coy
31 do " 2/Lt PRIDMORE killed. 4 men wounded.
During the month 2/Lt TAYLOR and ... fighting strength 31st Aug 21 Officers 522 OR.

21/WYR *War Diary* 25 – 31 August 1918

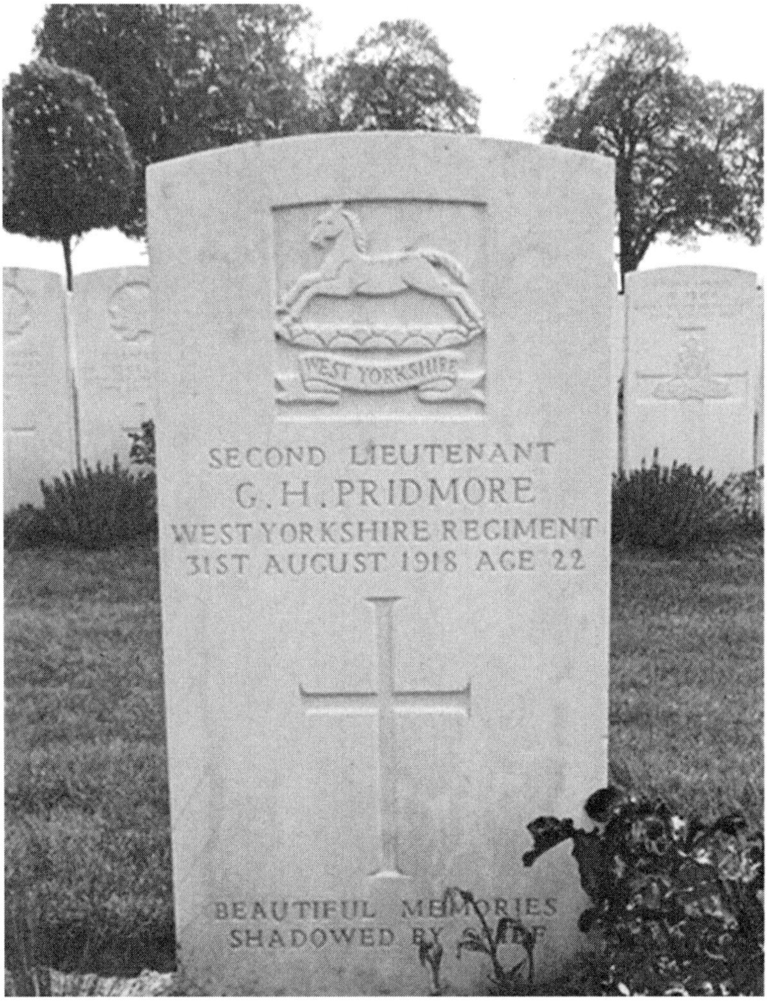

George's Headstone at Feuchy Chapel British Cemetery, Wancourt
(Courtesy George Horner)

The Pridmore Brothers Who Survived the Great War

'Discharged soldier out of work.'[188]

Ernest William Pridmore (1877–1948)

Of all the Pridmore brothers who survived childhood, only Ernest William, the oldest brother and William and Sarah's first born, didn't serve in the British Army; he was also their only child not to be born in Sheffield. Ernest married Elizabeth Ann Waters on 23 December 1900 and they had eight children, six of them girls, contrary to the common trait amongst the wider Pridmore family of predominantly male offspring. Two of their children died in infancy: Eliza (b. 4 November 1903–d. 30 May 1905) and Ernest (b. 2 June 1914–d. 7 November 1914). Eliza died of measles nephritis and Ernest junior died of bronchopneumonia. Both were buried in the same grave at Burngreave Cemetery.[189]

There are a number of reasons that could have possibly determined Ernest remaining a civilian. First, he may well not have passed fit enough to enlist; there was a history of ill health in his childhood and he was 37 years old when the War began, close to the upper age limit for the Army. However, he was within the age limits of 18 to 41 when conscription was introduced in 1916. It is also possible that by the time hostilities began, he was in a reserved occupation in the Sheffield steel or armaments industries. From the 1921 census, we find Ernest was out of work but had previously been a foundry worker at Hadfields East Hecla Works, which was largely engaged in producing war material, including the 14" Heclon armour-piercing shell and Era cast steel used in warship armour

[188] From 1921 census returns for both Oswald and Sidney Pridmore.

[189] Section Q, Grave 51

plating. His 19-year-old son William was also out of work, and he, too, had previously worked at Hadfields.

Ernest Pridmore (right) at his daughter Nellie's wedding, daughter Elizabeth is the bridesmaid. (Courtesy Maureen Ashe, Nellie's daughter)

Whatever the reason for Ernest not joining up, the deaths of his four brothers affected him deeply, perhaps leaving a feeling of guilt for not serving with them. In conversation with his granddaughter, Maureen Ashe, she told me that she remembers her grandad disappearing into his bedroom on Armistice Day and not reappearing until the following day; his way of dealing with his emotions and in remembering John, Albert, Arthur and George. Elizabeth Ann died in March 1928, aged 51, and Ernest William died in October 1948, aged 71. Both were buried in Burngreave Cemetery.[190]

[190] Section MM, Grave number 2637

Ernest's daughters: (left to right) Nellie, Lilian, Elizabeth, Rose and Hilda
(Courtesy Maureen Ashe)

The other three Pridmore brothers, Wilfred, Oswald and Sidney, also served in the Army; two of them fought in the War, and both were wounded.

Hadfields advertisement highlighting the possible reason
that Ernest was needed at work and not at war

Wilfred Pridmore (1892–1921)

Wilfred was the oldest of the three, and he enlisted in the York & Lancaster Regiment on 25 August 1914, before Albert joined the Regiment and before John and Arthur were killed; George would have finished his initial training but still would be in England. Following his training, Private 11039 Wilfred Pridmore was assigned to the 6th Battalion Y&LR, one of Lord Kitchener's New Army Battalions, and joined the War on 11 July 1915. According to his War Medal Card, he first saw action in the Balkans theatre. The Battalion sailed from Liverpool and landed at Suvla Bay in Gallipoli on 6 and 7 August 1915, as part of the 32nd Brigade in the 11th (Northern) Division.

On 19 and 20 December 1915, 6/Y&LR were evacuated from Gallipoli and moved to Egypt, where they took over a section of the Suez Canal defences on 19 February 1916, before moving on to the Western Front in July 1916. By 29 July, 6/Y&LR were in the Front Line at the Somme, taking part in the capture of the Wundt-Werk redoubt, the Battle Flers-Courcelette (15–27 September), and the Battle of Thiepval (26 September). Here, Wilfred was wounded and admitted to the Number 8 General Hospital at Rouen on 3 October, along with 130 other ranks and 40 officers that day.

This appears to be the end of Wilfred's war in France, as his wound was a 'Blighty', and he was returned to England, where he was transferred to the 150 Provisional Company of the Royal Defence Corps, [191] which was the London district, with a new service number: 64563. It is likely that his wounds rendered him unfit for active service and had contributed to his early discharge on 28 May 1918, as, in addition to his three War medals, he was also awarded the Silver War Badge, awarded to servicemen and women who were discharged during the War for reasons of no longer being physically fit to serve.

Wilfred was married before he enlisted, having wed Chloris Gertrude Moorhouse at St Stephen's Church, Netherthorpe, on 5 October 1913. At this time, Wilfred was employed as a carter. I have found no record of Wilfred and

---

[191] The Royal Defence Corps was set up by a Royal Warrant of 17 March 1916 and by Army Order 115 of 19 March 1916, to 'carry out duties connected with the local defence of the United Kingdom, including those hitherto performed by the Supplementary Territorial Force Companies, as well as those allotted to the Observers Companies now in process of formation.

Chloris having any children, and following Wilfred's death of pneumonia and asthenia in Lodge Moor Hospital on 8 March 1921, Chloris is living alone at 15 Silver Street, declaring that she had no dependents in the census returns of 19 June that year.

Wilfred died just four days short of his 29th birthday. He was working as a file stripper at the time of his death and living at his sister Lilian's house at 10 Brough Street; perhaps Wilfred and Chloris had separated before he died, as Chloris gives her address as 15 Silver Street when registering Wilfred's death.

Chloris died of ovarian cancer on 25 May 1933 at the City General Hospital (now Northern General Hospital), aged 41. At the time, she was living at 18 Havelock Square, Broomhall. She was buried at Burngreave Cemetery on 31 May 1933,[192] but in a different grave to that of Wilfred, who was buried on 14 March 1921.[193]

We don't know if Wilfred's War wounds contributed to his early death, but it is possible. If this were the case, we can say that not four but five Pridmore brothers died due to their fighting in the Great War.

The Silver War Badge

Oswald Pridmore (1893–1967)

Oswald Pridmore enlisted on 20 December 1915, which means that he volunteered before the Military Service Act of 1916, which made all single men

---

192 Section JJ, Grave 3089

193 Wilfred was buried in Section HH, Grave 5519

between the ages of 18 and 41 liable for military service. Oswald joined the 144th (York) Heavy Battery of the Royal Garrison Artillery and did see action in the War. The 144th HB sailed from Southampton alongside the Canadian Corps Heavy Artillery, arriving at Le Havre at 4.00am on 18 June 1916. From there, the two batteries moved by train to a position at Ypres, where they received their first German Shells on 24 June. Oswald's War Medal Card shows that he received the Victory Medal and the British War Medal. His Army Pension records also inform us that he received a gunshot wound to his hip, attributed by service, classing him as having a disability. From his medical records, we find that part of his femur was removed due to infection, and he was categorised 40% disabled. Oswald was discharged from service on 29 March 1920. He stayed a bachelor, living with his parents at 34 Hunt Street until they had both passed away. He was still at Hunt Street when, at 50 years old, he married 42-year-old spinster Annie Elizabeth Askham on 9 September 1944 at the Sheffield Registry Office. The 1939 Register records his occupation as a builders' labourer but, by 1944, he was a gas worker. It is no surprise that no record of any children is found. Oswald Pridmore died on 24 October 1967 and Annie in 1978.

Sidney Pridmore (1900–1982)

Sidney enlisted on 5 June 1918. Like John, Arthur and George, he first joined KOYLI but he later moved to the York & Lancaster Regiment, Albert's Regiment. From his Army Records, we find that he was 5' 6" tall, of fresh complexion, with hazel eyes and brown hair. He served for two years and 350 days, being discharged on 20 May 1921. It is unlikely that Private 4736814 Sidney Pridmore saw active service in the War, as he would have only just finished his training by the War's end, and he received no War Medals. Sidney's grandson, Alan Pridmore, relates that he served in Mesopotamia, now Iraq, probably after hostilities had ceased. We know from his War Medal Card that he was awarded the General Service Medal with North West Persia Clasp, which was for serving with the North Persia Force between 10 August 1920 and 31 December 1920. This meant Sidney was in the 2nd Battalion York & Lancaster Regiment, which formed part of the 51st Brigade of the 17th Division, sent to Iraq in 1919 to help defend Britain's interests in the area. A certificate of character issued on Sidney's discharge stated that he *'was very good, hardworking, honest and sober'*. On the 1921 census returns, both Oswald and

Sidney are recorded as *'discharged soldiers out of work'*. On 11 April 1922, Sidney married an expectant 22-year-old Catherine Violet Millership, the daughter of John Thomas Millership from Walton in Derbyshire, a boot and shoe repairer and later an engineer's turner/mechanical fitter. In 1922, they were living at 248 Penistone Road, and Sydney was now a railway porter. By 1940, he had moved job to being a shunter, still on the railway. They moved into 72 Robey Street in 1923 and remained there until at least October 1946. As prolific at procreation as the average Pridmore family were, they had at least eleven children between 1922 and 1946: William Thomas (b.18 September 1922), Arthur Edward (b.8 November 1923), Sydney (b.7 March 1926), Catherine (b.24 July 1924), twins Michael and Philip (b.2 November 1929), Lawrence (b.27 January 1931), Samuel Bernard (b.8 March 1934), Cyril (b.8 January 1936), Robert (b.2 January 1940), George (b.28 September 1946). There was also a stillborn birth in August 1937; buried in Burngreave Cemetery, the child was recorded as having died at 72 Robey Street.[194] Just one of the eleven children died in childhood: one of the twins, 5-year-old Philip, born 2 November 1929, died of diphtheria in December 1934.[195] Recollections from Michael's family suggest that Sydney, his older brother, had diphtheria at the same time as Philip but was put into isolation and survived. Philip was put in a general ward and succumbed to the disease.[196] Michael, on the other hand, lived the longest of any of the Pridmore family, dying on 6 January 2022 at the age of 92. Catherine died on 4 February 1960 and Sidney died on 4 March 1982.

It is interesting to note that two of their sons were named after Arthur and George.

---

[194] The child was buried in Section L1, Grave 46

[195] On the family website (http://family.nikellom.com/g2/p1195.htm#i29870), Michael Pridmore is also recorded as died a child but according to the family Michael lived until a few years ago.

[196] Information via Alan Pridmore.

Catherine Pridmore, nee Millership (left), Sidney Pridmore c1944 (centre) and Sydney junior with Oswald, 'uncle Oz' (courtesy Sue Rydiard and Alan Pridmore)

The Pridmore Sisters

Having introduced all of the Pridmore brothers, it is only right and proper to acquaint the reader with their sisters: Florence, Beatrice Eliza and Lilian May.

Florence Pridmore was born on 8 April 1885, probably at 4 Harleston Street, Burngreave. In 1901, the 15-year-old Florence was working as a fork and spoon buffer. Whilst living at 143 Daisy Walk, she married John William ('James') Palmer, a carter, on 2 August 1908 at St Stephen Church, Netherthorpe. John's name appears as James on the 1911 census returns and on their first child's birth certificate. Their son, also named James William, was born on 17 May 1909 at 34 Hunt Street. Their second son, Norman, was born on 17 October 1911 back at 143 Daisy Walk, but sadly died aged 10 years in the Royal Infirmary in October 1922. He was buried at Burngreave Cemetery on 11 October 1922.[197]

Their third child, Jennie, was born on 17 June 1914 at 10 Brough Street, Hillfoot. Jennie would marry Alfred Dalziel on 26 december 1936 at St John's Church, Owlerton; they were neighbours on Burnell Road, Jennie at number 1 and Alfred at number 11. Her father, who had joined the Army and fought in the War, was at the wedding, but Florence had died of influenza and pneumonia on 13 May 1920. She was buried at Burngreave Cemetery on 19 May 1920, in the same grave as Norman.[198]

From the 1921 census, we find that 36-year-old John (recorded as James) was now working as a stableman at Henry Tomlinson's Anchor Brewery on Cherry Street, Sheffield. Now a widower, he was living with his two remaining children at 10 Brough Street. Also at 10 Brough Street were his sister-in-law,

---

[197] Section HH, Grave 5519

[198] Her brother Wilfred would join them in this grave the following year.

Lilian, and her family. Lilian no doubt looked after the children whilst John was at work. However, on 20 March 1926, James married 40-year-old spinster Fanny Thornton at the Sheffield Registry Office. He was still employed as a stableman, and Fanny moves in with him at 10 Brough Street.

Banner advertisement for Henry Tomlinson's Anchor Brewery on Cherry Street

As we have seen in Chapter 1, Beatrice Eliza Pridmore died in infancy of pneumonia aged 22 months in 1889 at 4 Edgar Street and was buried at Burngreave Cemetery on 4 April.[199]

Lilian May Pridmore was born on 12 May 1889, a little over a month after Beatrice had been buried. In 1911, she was working as a live-in domestic servent for 50-year-old John Henry Bennett, publisher, and his family at 99 Broomspring Lane.[200] She married John Charles May on Christmas Day 1917 at St Stephen Church, where her elder sister had wed nine years previously. John was the younger brother of Margaret Pridmore, Albert's widow. Lilian and John had four children: Charles William, born 4 November 1918; Florence, born 8 November 1919; Lilian, born 31 March 1921; and Mary Ann, born 25 October 1922.

Once more, the curse of infant mortality struck the family, as Charles William died in Lodge Moor Hospital aged 18 months. He was buried at Burngreave Cemetery on 21 May 1920.[201] Lilian lived for just 17 days and died at 10 Brough Street, as Lilian and John were now living there with John Palmer and his children. The baby Lilian was buried at Burngreave Cemetery on 20 April 1921, just two days after John registered her birth; perhaps he registered her death at the same time.[202]

---

[199] Section C, Grave 79

[200] Today (2025) 99 Broomspring Lane is a 7 bedroom student accommodation house.

[201] Section S9, Grave 11

[202] Section BB, Grave 406

From the 1921 census, we find that John Charles May was working at Hadfields East Hecla Works as a joiner's labourer. He died in 1927, aged 40, at 72 Robey Street, the home of his brother-in-law Sidney and his family. He was buried on 11 June at Burngreave Cemetery.[203]

Florence did survive childhood and was certainly alive in 1944, when she was a witness at her uncle Oswald's wedding on 9 September that year.

I have been unable to find any further information about Mary Ann, other than that she was named after John's mother, and from the photo the family have found of her, she appears to have joined the military, probably during the Second World War.

Florence

[203] Section MM, Grave 2188. This is also the grave of Sidney's 5-year-old son Philip. Also in this grave is Mary Ann May, John Charles's mother, who was buried on 20 July 1928, a widow aged 62. She was living at 18 Marsden Lane.

Mary Ann May (Courtesy of Sue Rydiard)

The Pridmore Widows

'I felt I didn't want to live.
I had no wish to live at all because
the world had come to an end for me.
I had lost all that I loved.'[204]

It would be remiss of me not to include a chapter on the widows of the Pridmore brothers, for they bore more than most at the deaths of their husbands, with the exception of Thomas and Sarah Pridmore, the brothers' parents, but theirs was a different loss and a different grief. Yes, they all lost loved ones and no great a loss is imaginable for both wife and parent but different nevertheless. For the widows of the fallen in the Great War, the loss would be much more than that of their loved ones. For most, it also meant the loss of financial security, as the War Widows' Pension was barely enough to survive on, especially if there were children. It may mean her losing her home and becoming dependent on the wider family or charity. Britain's official charity for War widows was the Royal Patriotic Fund Corporation (RPFC), which dealt with cases where widows had been refused a pension. The RPFC would consider giving allowances where it thought appropriate. At the start of the War, the RPFC gave War widows £5 on the death of their husbands and an additional £1 for each child within the household.[205]

---

[204] Kitty Eckersley, whose husband Percy was killed at the Battle of the Somme in 1916: *www.thepastisaforeignpantry.com*

[205] Hetherington, Andrea, *British Widows of the First World War – The Forgotten Legion*, Pen & Sword Military, Barnsley, 2018, p. 56.

Even those who were lucky enough to receive a pension found themselves much worse off financially than before the War. A study undertaken by the National Council for Social Services (NCSS), set up in 1920, found that there were 22% of families with no other source of income but the pension, and that they were surviving on half of their pre-war income.[206] The option of finding a job wasn't feasible for widows with children unless the wider family helped with childcare. And whilst for some, where jobs were available during the War years, on cessation of hostilities, things changed dramatically as demobilised soldiers returned to the labour market, reducing opportunities and, in some cases, women losing their jobs to be replaced by the men. Some widows found themselves with no other option but to apply for Poor Law relief. Of those studied by the NCSS, 35% of widows were in receipt of Poor Law relief.[207] There were numerous possibilities of a widow's fate, few of them good. I have tried to find out as much as I can about the fate of the Pridmore widows and how their lives panned out following the loss of their soldier husbands.

On 14 October 1914, Harriet Annie Pridmore became a widow, and the infants Ernest, Gladys and Frederick lost their father. There were no War widows' pensions until early 1915. The Ministry of Pensions was established in 1916, and even then, not all women who lost their husbands in the War got a pension. They would have to face assessment by the Special Grants Committee, which would take into account their moral character as part of their assessment. In 1914, a War widow not only lost her husband and the father of her children, she also lost her breadwinner and source of security. If not in receipt of support from her wider family, life would be very difficult, especially if she had young children to care for. If she couldn't find work, she had to find another husband.

From the records, we find that Harriet received a pension of 20/6[208] per week from 19 April 1915. I initially thought that Harriet would also receive an allowance for each of her three children, but the pension approval document lists the names of the children as inclusive of the claim. The children's allowances ended on their respective sixteenth birthdays. By the end of the War, almost 200,000 widows and 330,000 children were receiving state pensions, but tens of

---

[206] Ibid., p. 44.

[207] Ibid, p. 47.

[208] 20/6 was 20 shillings and 6 old pennies, also written as 20s-6d in pre-decimal currency. 20 shillings was £1, so could also be written as £1-0s-6d.

thousands got no support at all; most relied on voluntary organisations and charity.[209]

Should a War widow remarry, she would forfeit her widow's pension but would receive a gratuity of two years' pension. After 1917, this was reduced to one year. She would still get the children's allowance up until their sixteenth birthday. Cohabitation would also result in the widow forfeiting her pension.

By the time of the 1921 census, Harriet and the three children were living in a two-roomed house at 2 Court, number 3 House, Ellison Street, Walkley, seemingly existing solely on her widow's pension and perhaps some support from one of the local charities such as the Salvation Army. Sometime after this, Harriet remarried another (ex) military man: Thomas Naylor Sharpe, a former Gunner in the Royal Garrison Artillery (RGA), who moved in with her at Ellison Street.

Thomas attested on 19 April 1915 and joined 137 Company, Royal Field Artillery (RFA), as Gunner 225807 and later moved to the RGA. The RGA provided the heaviest of the British Artillery and was generally situated farthest away from the front line, still within range of the German Artillery but less of a target and with safer prospects than the infantry in the trenches. Thomas was discharged in consequence of demobilisation on 28 August 1920 and was awarded the 1914–15 Star, British War Medal and the Victory Medal: *'Pip, Squeak & Wilfred'*.[210]

Harriet also outlived Thomas, as he died in May 1933, aged 49. I have his three medals on display at home, along with John's medals and bronze death plaque; John's '*Pip*' is the Mons Star, bearing the dates August and November 1914.

By 1939, Harriet was living alone in a flat at 10 Kyle Close. At this time, she was working as a paid domestic cleaner. She died in March 1944, aged 57. My grandfather, her son Ernest William Pridmore, found her dead in bed when visiting her at Kyle Close. Thomas and Harriet are buried together in grave number 19687, section A6, City Road Cemetery, Sheffield.

---

209 https://historywm.com/films/hidden-home-front-war-widows-pensions-episode-7

210 The nicknames of the three WWI medals that came about due to the popularity of three cartoon characters in a Daily Mirror cartoon strip, which appeared in 1919.

Harriet Annie Pridmore Gunner 225807 Thomas Naylor Sharpe

John's and Thomas's Medals and John's 'Death Penny'

By the time that she got her widow's pension on 24 May 1915, Annie Elizabeth Pridmore was living at 65 Avenue Street at Tanshelf in Pontefract, although there are a number of addresses written then crossed out on the pension approval document: Corporation Buildings, Halfpenny Lane; 49 South Avenue, Pontefract; 65 Avenue Mount, Pontefract; and the last, which wasn't crossed out, was simply Womersley, New Doncaster, which is a small village to the east of Pontefract. She was awarded a pension of 13/6 per week. On 1 November 1915, Annie enrolled and undertook the Central Midwives Board examination, which she passed. We also find from the records that, in 1917, Annie received a grant of £10 to pay for her to train as a General Nurse at the West Riding Nursing Asylum at Leeds for three months. This was later increased by another £5 to extend the course to 6 months. Having lost her husband and a brother-in-law early in the War, and perhaps now knowing that another brother-in-law, Albert, had died of his wounds in Bradford Hospital and of course another brother-in-law, George Harry, was now fighting in France, she wanted to make her own contribution to the war effort and to help other wounded soldiers in their recovery. I'd like to think that she wanted to do her bit. After all, she was born into a military family and had moved to Pontefract, where she was near the Pontefract Barracks, home of the York & Lancaster Regiment. However, it would appear that her interest lay in helping other women, as we find her on the 1926 Midwives Roll, and she is living at 72 Westwood Terrace, The Mount, York. For some reason, she doesn't appear on the 1921 census returns. Having no children, there was no one to hand down the family history, and with her not living near the wider Pridmore family, after her taking up midwifery in York in 1926, the trail runs dry until we find her death on 9 November 1934, aged 59. She was living at Maple Avenue, Bishopthorpe, and probate records show that she left an estate of £576-10s, the equivalent of £52,727 at today's value (2025). We can also discern from this record that she didn't remarry.

Albert's wife, Margaret, applied for her War Widow's Pension in July 1917, and her application showed that she was living at 71 Hollis Croft, Sheffield, with her four children. She was awarded 28/9 per week from 24 December 1917. Again, this included allowances for each of the four children. It is interesting to note the comment *'Born before wedlock'* under the names of the eldest three on the pension approval document. Margaret spent the rest of her life at Hollis Croft, where she had an illegitimate child on 21 October 1919; a boy that she named John William Pridmore. In 1921, like Harriet, she was living with her now five children and existing solely on her widow's pension. She died at Firvale Hospital, Herries Road, in January 1931, aged 47. She was buried with Albert and their tragic son, Albert Junior, at Burngreave Cemetery.

Back in 1911, George's future wife, the 15-year-old May Foster, was living in the family two-up and two-down terraced home at 9 Burton Street with her parents, William and Kate Eliza Foster, and three brothers: 19-year-old Fred, 17-year-old Sydney and 9-year-old Harry. A typical Sheffield working-class family, they were all employed in the steel industry in one form or another. William was a roll turner, maybe working at one of the local rolling mills on Penistone Road. Fred was a steel rod roller. Again, there were local mills where he could have been working. Similarly, Sydney, a sheet roller, could have been working nearby. May, too, was working with steel as an engineering machine minder. From the 1911 census returns, we learn that May had two other siblings who were no longer at home, so likely to be older. We also learn that she had two siblings who had died. Like many families at the time, as we have seen with the Pridmores, the Fosters may have lost two children to death in infancy.

Hollis Croft, late 19th century

A Hollis Croft courtyard

At the time of George's death, May was living at 10 Exley Avenue, Walkley, a three-bedroom terrace house. This was May's address entered on the couple's marriage certificate and so likely to have been the Foster family home when they married. George, having been killed just two days short of their first wedding anniversary, and most of that year spent in France and Belgium, the couple had little opportunity to set up a home of their own.

Being married to an officer, May Pridmore's War Pension was determined by a different allowances system. Information is found in the War Office Widows of Army Officers records. For May, we find that she was entitled to an annual gratuity of £100[211] from 11 September 1918. This was paid to her in monthly amounts that varied. She received her first payment of £8-3s-1d on 7 November 1918, with another payment of £8 on the same date; this would cover the one month's arrears. In December, she received £8 and another £9 in January 1919. By April 1919, she had received £58. Over the next twelve months, she received a sequence of £8 for two months and £14 in the third month. This is

[211] £100 in 1918 is the equivalent of £4,775.06 in August 2024: Bank of England Inflation Calculator.

repeated for the next three quarters, and when added up, the annual payment was £120. I have only seen the records for 1918–1920, and I can only assume that these payments continued in the following years. These records also show that by 17 February 1920, May had moved to 129 Whitehouse Lane, Walkley.

George had completed the Army's Will form on 30 June 1916, following his initial posting to France, in which he left his property and effects to his mother, Sarah Jane Pridmore. After getting married, this Will was withdrawn, and although not replaced by an updated Will in respect of May, his estate would eventually be granted to May by Letter of Administration on 23 April 1919. The gross value of George's estate amounted to £95-6s-9d. This included £58-10s-8d of George's Army effects.

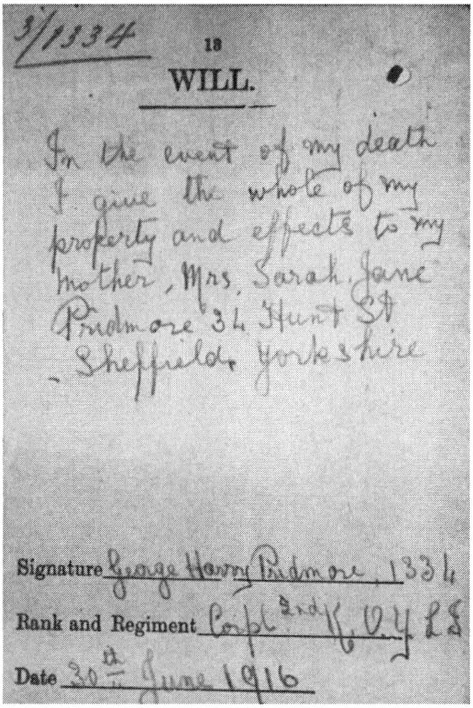
3/1334 18

WILL.

In the event of my death I give the whole of my property and effects to my mother, Mrs. Sarah Jane Pridmore 34 Hunt St Sheffield, Yorkshire

Signature George Harry Pridmore, 1334

Rank and Regiment Corpl 2nd K.O.Y.L.I.

Date 30th June 1916

George's early Army Will

Although George's effects had been determined by the War Office Standing Committee of Adjustment, who would have paid off any of George's debts before finalising George's credit in his Army account, there later appeared a perceived discrepancy of £15-15s in May's calculation, or that of a friend of George that she was in contact with. On 15 September 1927, she wrote to the

War Office suggesting that this said amount had been stopped twice, once from his bank account and again from his allowances. It would appear that this was a misunderstanding on May's and this friend of George's part, as the reply that she received from the War Office, dated 24 September, stated that the £15-15s was actually credited to his account and not debited; it was pay in advance which was then deducted from the total of George's effects. The letter ended with, *'No amount is now due to the deceased's estate from Army funds'*.

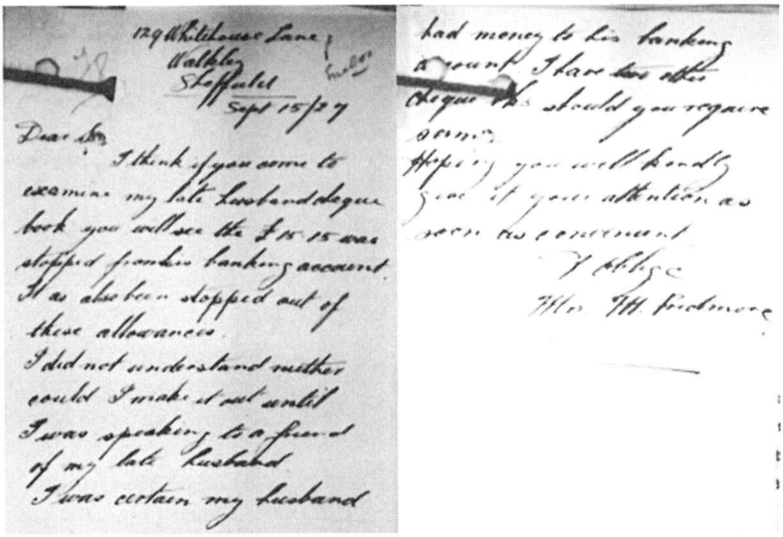
129 Whitehouse Lane
Walkley
Sheffield
Sept 15/27

Dear Sir
I think if you come to examine my late husband's cheque book you will see the £15 15 was stopped from his banking account. It as also been stopped out of these allowances.
I did not understand neither could I make it out until I was speaking to a friend of my late husband.
I was certain my husband had money to his banking account. I have two other cheques should you require some.
Hoping you will kindly give it your attention as soon as convenient.
Y Oblige
Mrs M. Pridmore

May's letter to the War Office, 15 September 1927

I think we can deduce that May used some of this money to move out of the Foster family home and into the three-bedroom terraced house at 129 Whitehouse Lane, Walkley, where she set up a boarding business. On the 1921 census form, she describes herself as *'Boarding House Keeper'* and listed in the occupants column are two boarders: 29-year-old Alfred Dearman and 8-month-old Desmond Wells. Alfred was an engineer's blacksmith working at Thomas Firth & Sons on Saville Street. Interestingly, he is a married man, but there is no mention of his wife. Being born at Owlerton, he was a local man and not someone who had moved to Sheffield for his work. And who is the infant Desmond Wells? According to the information on the census form, both of his parents are alive, and he was born in Sheffield—another Pridmore family mystery.

On 29 July 1922, May gave birth to an illegitimate baby girl who she named Barbara May Pridmore. According to the Baptism record, the father was Alfred Dearman.[212] It would seem that May, although still living at 129 Whitehouse Lane, had given up the boarding house business, as the Registrar had recorded on the birth certificate that May was *'of no occupation'*.

In the 1939 Register, we find that May has remarried and is living in a spacious semi-detached house at 555 Herries Road. May married 38-year-old Leonard Elliott in 1934, and they share the house with May's daughter, Barbara May, now 17 years old and working as a milliner's shop assistant, and May's brother, Harry, now a steelworker.

Now entering the period of the Second World War, on 11 December 1943, we find that Barbara May Pridmore married 25-year-old John Foster, a Lance Sergeant in the British Army living at 33 Tavistock Road, at the Abbeydale Methodist Church. Barbara, now 21, was working as a munitions worker. The most interesting thing about the recording of the marriage was in the column for the fathers' names on the marriage certificate; Barbara's father's name is given as George Harry Pridmore (Deceased). Of course, George Harry Pridmore was deceased four years before Barbara's birth; God works in mysterious ways!

I touched earlier on the class dimension to the British Army, and it is further emphasised with the inequalities in the allocation of War Pensions, comparing the widows of officers with those of other ranks. Annie Elizabeth and May Pridmore are comparable with their losses, as neither widow had children to support, yet Annie received a pension amounting to £32-8s per annum compared to May's £100. The reader will also note that there is more information available on officers than there is on other ranks.

---

[212] *http://www.sheffieldindexers.com/ParishBaptismIndex.html.* Barbara was Baptised at All Saints Church, Brightside, on 16 August 1922.

The Pridmore Children

'Suffer little children,
and forbid them not,
to come unto me.'[213]

It is estimated that around 360,000 British children lost their fathers in the Great War. Research has found that these children, and those whose fathers came home seriously wounded, died on average a year younger than their counterparts. The same study found that the life expectancy of those who became fatherless whilst still in the womb was reduced by more than two years. It is believed that this was due to the impact of the psychological stress suffered by mothers and their children.[214] A year doesn't seem a lot, but life expectancy in Britain in 1914 was only 51 years for men and 55 years for women. As we know, infant mortality rates in Britain were high at the time, and they varied between social classes, with unskilled labourers losing 152 infants per 1,000 live births, compared to 133 per 1,000 in working-class families. To emphasise the social inequalities at the time, middle- and upper-class families' infant deaths were 77 per 1,000—less than half of the unskilled labouring class. To put these figures into context, the infant mortality rate in the UK in 2021 was just 4 deaths per 1,000 live births.[215] So, how did the surviving Pridmore children, who lost their father in the War, fare?

---

[213] Matthew 19:14

[214] Todd, Nicolas, *The Epidemiological Consequences of War*, video lecture on ultv.univ-lorraine.fr

[215] *www.statista.com/statistics/281501/infant-mortality-rate-in-the-united-kingdom/*

Of the four Pridmore brothers killed in the War, only John and Albert were fathers, and between them they had ten children, but only seven survived the War; two of Albert's offspring dying in infancy long before the War began, and Albert Junior tragically being killed at work, aged just 14, in 1915.

John's eldest was my grandfather, Ernest William, who was just six years old when John went off to France. Next was Gladys, who was four, and then Frederick, a little over a year old. All three lived more than the three score years and ten, and there is no evidence to suggest that the length of their lives were affected by the loss of their father; only Ernest would have any lasting memory of John. The three of them were brought up by Harriet and later also by their stepfather, Thomas Sharpe.

Ernest William, known as 'Bill', married my grandmother, Lilian Elizabeth Redfern, daughter of steelworks labourer Thomas Redfern, on 18 December 1926; Thomas Sharpe was a witness. Lilian was born at Court 2, Allen Street, on 13 September 1907. Her mother, Mary Redfern, registered the birth on 5 November 1907. Ernest and Lilian had two children, both girls, separated by 10 years. My mother, Jean, was born on 1 October 1931 at 14 Parkwood Road, Neepsend, and her sister, Betty, was born on 27 July 1941 at 14 Lamb Road, Parson Cross; the propensity not to settle anywhere seems to have been inherited down the lineage. Lilian died of breast cancer on 19 January 1959 in the Royal Infirmary. I am Jean's only child, but Betty had four children: two boys and two girls.

Gladys married 21-year-old labourer Norman Nicholson on 2 February 1929 at York Registry Office. Gladys was 22 and living at 7 Fishergate, York. Norman was living at 18 Baxter Avenue in Haworth. They had five children: Jimmy, Alan, Sheila, Mavis and John. Gladys died in September 2001 in York.

Frederick married 17-year-old Doris Harrison on 25 February 1933 at the Sheffield Registry Office. He was a 19-year-old engineer's turner living at 51 Ball Street. Doris was living at 32 Hanworth Street. They had three children: Maureen (b. 1933–d. 18 December 1978), Kenneth (b. November 1938) and Sylvia (b. c 1940–d. 6 March 2008). Frederick died in Sheffield on 29 January 1991 and is buried in City Road Cemetery.

Ernest William Pridmore giving daughter Jean away, 22 December 1951 (author's collection)

Gladys, Ernest William (Bill) and Betty, early 1980s (author's collection)

Fred and Doris Pridmore's children: Maureen, Sylvia and Ken, 4 October 1940

Harriet with her first grandson, Jimmy Nicholson, 9 June 1930

Albert's surviving children were George (b. 11 January 1907–d. 1978), Ernest (b. 4 November 1908–d. c August 1989), Harold (b. 13 December 1910–d. c May 1972) and Mary (b. 5 March 1914–d. c March 1993). At 3 years old, only Mary would have little memory of her father, but his three sons would remember him well enough, and they would have understood that they would not see their father again. Compounded by the death of their big brother a couple of years previously, the news of Albert having died of his wounds at Bradford would have had a traumatic effect on them and their emotions. We can well imagine how this would have brought them closer to their mother, and how they would have thought how unfair their situation was, and how unfair was the hand that the family had been dealt, for they would also be aware of the earlier deaths of their uncles John and Arthur.

Ernest Pridmore was still living with his mother at 71 Hollis Croft in July 1930, but later moved to Romford in Essex, where he married Charlotte Ruth Allen, 'Lottie', the daughter of John and Lottie Allen, née Theaker. They had three children: John Ernest, Patricia Mary and Barbara Joan. Ernest died in Havering, Essex, in August 1989, aged 80.

Ernest Pridmore, Albert's son (Courtesy Barbara Bobrowicz, Ernest's daughter)

Harold married Eva Synyer on 22 April 1933, and they had two boys: Raymond (b.16 November 1933–d. 3 October 1998), Gordon (b.17 November 1937–d. August 2001). In 1911, Eva was living in the Sheffield Union Children's Home at Smilter Lane, Pitsmoor; she may have been born in the Workhouse. At the time of their marriage, Harold was living with his mother at 71 Hollis Croft and worked as a painter's palette knife hafter. Eva was also living in Hollis Croft, at 20 Court, number 4 House. They moved to 18 Morgan Avenue, Parson Cross. Eva died in the Nether Edge Hospital on 29 August 1959, aged 49. She was buried at City Road Cemetery, Sheffield.[216]

On 24 December 1960, Harold, still living at Morgan Avenue, re-married to 51-year-old widow Annie Burns, née Oxley, of 28 Ronald Road, a two-bedroom terraced house off Staniforth Road. It was recorded on the marriage certificate that Harold was now working as a fettler at a steelworks, and Annie was a carriage painter. It was also a surprise to note that Harold's father's occupation (Albert) is recorded as steeplejack (journeyman); another Pridmore mystery. Witness to the marriage was Harold's brother George. Harold died in May 1972, aged 61.

Wedding of Harold and Annie; left to right: George Pridmore, Harold, Annie and second witness Mrs M Marsden (Courtesy Paul and Raymond Pridmore, Harold's grandsons)

[216] City Road Cemetery, Section MM, Row 7, Grave number 14137

Harold Pridmore with son Raymond and grandson, Raymond junior, on VE Day 1955
(Courtesy Ray Pridmore junior)

Mary was living with her mother at 71 Hollis Croft in 1933, but she later married Horace Tompkins at the Holy Trinity Church on the corner of Nursery Street and Johnson Street on 23 August 1941. They had a daughter, Mary, who married a man called Fox. Mary died a widow on 27 February 1993 at Chapeltown Nursing Home on Steven Crescent, Chapeltown, aged 79. I have found no information about Horace other than that he died a retired cutler, as did Mary. The cause of death was carcinomatosis, primary carcinoma (no site specified), and Parkinson's disease. I understand that daughter Mary Fox had three children: David, Jennifer and Gillian.

One note of interest is that Ernest and Mary were both baptised, not as children but at 23 and 19 years of age respectively—Ernest on 26 July 1930 and Mary on 1 July 1933, both at St Vincent's Catholic Church on White Croft. I have found no other reference to any of the Pridmores being Catholic.

It was during the 1930s that many of the old back-to-back houses on and around the Sheffield Crofts were demolished in a Sheffield Council slum-clearance programme, with many of the locals having to move away from the area. This may be one of the reasons for some of the family losing contact with others as they moved to new homes, perhaps some distance away.

Hollis Croft with St Vincent's in the background, c.1910

Overdue Recognition

When you go home, tell them of us and say,
For your tomorrow, we gave our today.[217]

I have been writing about the Pridmore brothers since I first became aware of their collective sacrifice, and that no other Sheffield family gave so much in the Great War. This is over twenty years ago. Letters and articles published in the local press over the years, and articles written by others in local magazines, failed to prompt anyone at the local authority to give some kind of civic recognition of the brothers and their family. Despite my disappointment at this indifference, I was not surprised. The subjects of my previous books are all aspects of Sheffield's history that have been understated, in my opinion, so why should the story of one family's contribution to the Great War be any different? Sheffield doesn't seem to appreciate its history or its heritage. Still, my perseverance eventually paid off after I wrote directly to Sheffield City Council (SCC), albeit after my letter had been passed around internally at the Town Hall. Eventually, it landed on the desk of Councillor Denise Fox, who was the Council's Armed Forces Champion, and at last, somebody at the Council recognised the significance of the Pridmore brothers' story.

It was in August 2022 that I was first contacted by an officer of the Council who told me that my submission was to be discussed at a forthcoming meeting and that I would be contacted again after said meeting.

Having been a council officer myself (not Sheffield), I am aware that internal bureaucracy and procedures do not equate to a quick decision-making process. Nevertheless, by the end of August, I was informed that the meeting had agreed to honour the brothers and that officers had been tasked with investigating the options.

---

[217] The Kohima Epitaph

By October, it had been decided that the Sheffield Midland Station be contacted with a view to getting their permission to install a plaque there, the reasoning for this being that most of Sheffield's soldiers would have entrained there when on their way to the War and it would have been their last view of Sheffield as they departed.

The wheels of the establishment move slowly, and it wasn't until August 2023 that some progress had been made. But it was at this point that the people at Midland Station had not only agreed to host the plaque, but a site for its installation had been identified, and, obviously, much had been discussed behind the scenes without any further input from me or any of the wider Pridmore family.

This was rectified when a meeting was arranged at Midland Station with Council officer Paul Taylor and members of the Pridmore family: Ben Pridmore, Sue Rydiard and I. This was the first time that I had met Ben, but I was familiar with his online blog on the Pridmore family, which had been invaluable for my own research.

We were able to present Paul Taylor with much information on the brothers, and Ben provided a family tree. This would be used to provide accessible background information for the public once the plaque had been unveiled, something that the railway people wanted to provide. We all felt the meeting was meaningful and removed any doubts that we had about the project's future; it was going to happen!

The next thing to sort out was the design of the plaque and what information was to go on it. Ben and Sue were happy for me to negotiate this on behalf of the family, which I did, keeping them informed along the way.

This took quite a prolonged exchange of emails between various interested parties, but was finally resolved when I met with Cllr Denise Fox at the Town Hall, where the reservations that I had were resolved. My reservations revolved around the plaque being specifically about the Pridmore brothers, rather than it being expanded as an all-embracing commemoration, as some would have had it.

It was at this meeting that Denise confidentially informed me that the plaque would be funded by four past Master Cutlers who wished to remain anonymous. No funding was provided by the Council, only officer time and expenses.

I felt that this was a wonderful gesture by the dignitaries, and I said so in my speech on the day of the unveiling. I also felt that Sheffield City Council was most disingenuous in its respect for the brothers.

Once the design had been agreed, the next thing was to organise an unveiling ceremony, which was undertaken by Denise, Midland Station representatives and the participating organisations. I was happy for them to undertake the task and it was eventually arranged for the event to take place on the Friday of Remembrance weekend, 10 November 2023.

On the day, it was a spectacular event, but I was disappointed to learn that the Lord Lieutenant and the Lord Mayor, who were programmed to do the unveiling, would not be in attendance. This was down to there being a Royal visit that clashed, which turned out to be to commemorate an elephant that was used in the steel works during the Great War; somehow, I felt that priorities had gone awry. In their place, Christopher Jowitt, the Deputy Lieutenant of South Yorkshire, did the unveiling, with proceedings being led by the Railway Chaplain. It was also notable that, despite the event being a commemoration of the Pridmore brothers, they didn't get a mention in the official programme.

Also, during the period between my first contact with SCC and the unveiling event, the Council were organising the installation of a plaque in recognition of the Sheffield tree protestors in the entrance of the Town Hall, at a reported estimated cost of £10,000. This was confirmed by Project Officer Dan Whittaker, who informed me that the Council's Strategy and Resources Policy Committee agreed the £10,000 for the project on 19 June 2023; priorities gone awry again, I suggest.[218]

Nevertheless, whoever did the unveiling didn't depreciate the contributions from the participants: Royal British Legion, the KOYLI Light Infantry and Rifles Regiment Association, the Prince of Wales Own Association, and the Minden House Buglers. The display of banners and the sound of the buglers made the atmosphere captivating. Speeches were made, including yours truly (see Appendix 6), prayers and exhortation delivered, culminating with a blessing and the National Anthem. The whole thing brought a sense of pride and a realisation that my efforts had all been worthwhile. Not only had the Pridmore brothers been given the recognition that they rightly deserved, but it brought together probably the biggest gathering of the wider Pridmore family, who attended from the length

[218] *The Sheffield Star*, 21 June 2023

and breadth of the country, ever to assemble. Like me, many were able to meet members of their family for the very first time.

Author speaking at the unveiling ceremony (Sheffield Star)

A Remembrance service was repeated at Sheffield Midland Station on 11 November 2024, when wreaths were laid under the Pridmore brothers' plaque, and being the only War memorial on site, this will be repeated annually. This means that the Pridmore brothers will be commemorated in perpetuity: Lest We Forget.

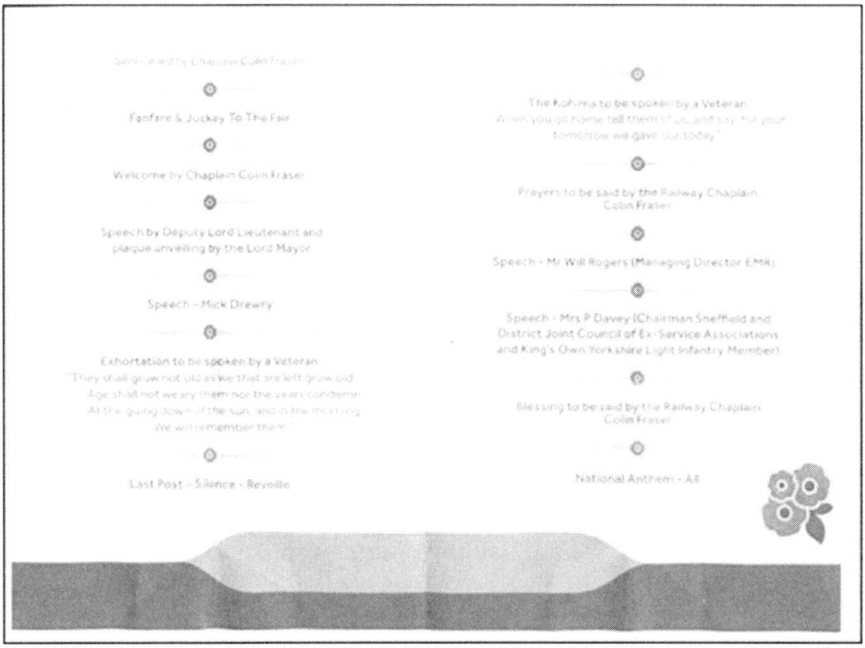

Service led by Chaplain Colin Fraser

Fanfare & Jockey To The Fair

Welcome by Chaplain Colin Fraser

Speech by Deputy Lord Lieutenant and plaque unveiling by the Lord Mayor

Speech – Mick Drewry

Exhortation to be spoken by a Veteran
"They shall grow not old as we that are left grow old
Age shall not weary them nor the years condemn
At the going down of the sun, and in the morning
We will remember them."

Last Post – Silence – Reveille

The Kohima to be spoken by a Veteran
"When you go home tell them of us and say, for your tomorrow we gave our today."

Prayers to be said by the Railway Chaplain Colin Fraser

Speech – Mr Will Rogers (Managing Director EMR)

Speech – Mrs P Davey (Chairman Sheffield and District Joint Council of Ex-Service Associations and King's Own Yorkshire Light Infantry Member)

Blessing to be said by the Railway Chaplain Colin Fraser

National Anthem – All

Unveiling event programme, 10 November 2023

Members of the Pridmore family attending the plaque unveiling, 10 November 2023 (Sheffield Star)

Conclusion

The migrant Pridmore family were typical of the 19th century when, living an impoverished life in rural Pickworth and Bourn with little opportunity for advancement, the temptation of socio-economic improvement perceived by the booming industries of Sheffield was succumbed to. But there was a price to pay, and the Pridmore family paid in extremes: the bad housing, overcrowding, pollution and poor sanitary conditions, with the resulting high level of infant mortality, tolled on generations of the family. The addition of losing four sons to the nadir of humanity that was paradoxically termed the *'Great War'* determined that the Pridmore family's story was not so typical; few fathers have suffered the grief of outliving ten of their thirteen children.

Although Albert wasn't keen to join the British Army, John, Arthur and George seem to have been attracted to a life in uniform; I do believe that they also had an avid sense of adventure. The British Army was in action in South Africa when John and Arthur enrolled, but their thoughts on actually being involved in war didn't put them off. As things turned out, only John found himself facing the bullets and shells of the Boers. We don't know how John's experiences impacted his emotions, but it gave him a foretaste of what was to come, something Arthur could only imagine when he was the first of the brothers to embark for France in 1914.

Arthur must have taken to life in the Army, as he stayed in after his obligatory six years and became a recruiting sergeant. Albert's change of heart may have been due to the loss of his two brothers in October 1914, for he did eventually volunteer in 1915, before conscription. George, on the other hand, was keen as mustard to join and was perhaps the most conscientious soldier of the brothers, despite his early disciplinary record. Certainly, his performance rewarded him with a quick succession of promotions, culminating in a commission, with two of these promotions being awarded in the field, which is meritorious in itself.

However, this last promotion was statistically fatal and proved to be so, although 2nd Lieutenant George Harry Pridmore survived more than the average six-week life expectancy of a subaltern on the Western Front.

Insofar as we can only imagine the experiences of the brothers in the field, we can picture the horrors of the War on the Western Front that most British soldiers faced and endured, as they are well illustrated in the official war records and the personal memoirs of the British Tommy. In this context, I have told the Pridmore brothers' war story through the war diaries of the battalions in which they served, which is about as close as we can get to understanding their experiences up until their deaths, or, in Albert's case, being wounded. Equally, we don't know how they died, but the options were horrendous. Perhaps Albert's death was the least bearable, having lingered for weeks in a hospital bed before succumbing to his wounds, the nature of which, again, we have no knowledge of.

In my research, it was only natural that I would come across the brothers' comrades who died alongside them as they fought and died, particularly those who were killed on the same day, perhaps by the same shell. Some would be friends as well as comrades-in-arms, perhaps close friends determined by the mutual circumstances that they found themselves in. I couldn't just gloss over these men, for they were more than asides or mere statistics; they were party to the story.

Knowing that four brothers died in the War is thought-provoking and we feel for their immediate families. Then, as the story unfolds, we find that four could have been six, or even seven. Wilfred and Oswald were fortunate not to have been amongst those killed in action, but merely wounded and then discharged from the Army. Sidney only just missed the action and served his country in Mesopotamia, seemingly without coming to any harm. I won't dwell on this, but I do wonder if the Pridmore brothers' story would have been told before now had their number been five, six or seven.

Following on from the brothers' lives, an extension to the Pridmore family history was a natural course for me to take so as to find how the widows and children fared. I'm sure that the reader would expect it; like me, they would hunger for more.

The Pridmore brothers' story needed to be told, and I am only sorry that I didn't write this book before my mother passed away in December 2020, for she would have been fascinated in the history of her family. Of course, this also applies to me and my children. We may not bear the Pridmore name, but we are immensely proud of our Pridmore heritage.

It took far too long for the four Pridmore brothers to be honoured by the Sheffield authorities, and whilst the family appreciate the plaque to commemorate them at Sheffield Midland Station, perhaps once the whole story is known to them, the city leaders will consider a memorial to the four Pridmore brothers of Sheffield who paid the ultimate sacrifice to defend our freedom—one that people would want to come and see when they visit, not simply pass on their way out of Sheffield. And perhaps Sheffield City Council will reflect on its decisions: not to give financial support for a memorial to the Pridmore brothers, then give £10,000 for a plaque to the tree protesters, and actually fund one.

Whilst this concludes my story of the Pridmore brothers, I am sure it will not be the end of their story, for when their descendants have read my account, it will entice many of them to look further into their own family linage and no doubt uncover more information, and undoubtedly more Pridmore mysteries, which will be a rewarding outcome for the author.

Appendix 1

2/KOYLI soldiers died near Pont Fixe on 14 October 1914

Private 7991 John William Howe, husband of Eliza Howe of 36 Ashley Lane, Killamarsh, North East Derbyshire, commemorated at Le Touret Memorial, Panel 31

Private 7869 Harry Jagger, aged 30, son of John Inkerman and Jane Jagger of 20 Charles Street, Swinton, Yorkshire, commemorated at Le Touret Memorial, Panel 31

Private 3/6696 Thomas Jennings, aged 37, brother of John W Jennings of 23 Cross Bedford Street, Sheffield, buried at Browns Road Military Cemetery, Festubert, Grave number V.A.8

Private 6640 John Thomas Pridmore, aged 33, son of William Thomas and Sarah Jane Pridmore of 34 Hunt Street, Netherthorpe, Sheffield; husband of Harriet Pridmore of 4/1 Hunt Street, Netherthorpe, Sheffield, commemorated at Le Touret Memorial, Panel 31

Lance Sergeant 10177 Ernest Smith, commemorated at Le Touret Memorial, Panel 31

Private 5706 George Harry Stones, aged 35, husband of J.E. Baines (formerly Stones) of 5 Hope Avenue, Goldthorpe, Rotherham, commemorated at Le Touret Memorial, Panel 31

Appendix 2

2/KOYLI soldiers died at Lannoy on 18 October 1914

Private 9272 Sidney Barringer, commemorated at Le Touret Memorial, Panel 31

Private 7983 George Bartlett, buried at Terlincthun British Cemetery, Wimille, Grave number VII.C.35

Private 6438 Frederick William Bettney, commemorated at Le Touret Memorial, Panel 31

Sergeant 6218 Harry James Boon, aged 29, son of Mr & Mrs W.H. Boon of 20 Ceres Road, Plumstead, London, buried at Canadian Cemetery No.2 Neuville-St Vaast, Grave number 15.J.21

Private 7135 Edward Cavell, commemorated at Le Touret Memorial, Panel 31

Private 10887 John Harry Cross, commemorated at Le Touret Memorial, Panel 31

Private 6657 Percy Crouch, aged 35, husband of Maria C Crouch of Station Road, Ryhill, Wakefield, commemorated at Le Touret Memorial, Panel 31

Private 10676 William Currie, commemorated at Le Touret Memorial, Panel 31

Private 8326 Joseph Derham, aged 28, son of Mr & Mrs James Derham of 10 Grove Place, Claypit Lane, Leeds, commemorated at Le Touret Memorial, Panel 31

Lance Corporal 9042 Albert Elson, commemorated at Le Touret Memorial, Panel 31

Private 8534 George Gale, commemorated at Le Touret Memorial, Panel 31

Private 7932 George Gollick, buried at Canadian Cemetery No.2 Neuville-St Vaast, Grave number 15.J.20

Private 5877 John Kelly, aged 34, husband of Sarah Ann Winter (formerly Kelly) of 8 Edmunds Road, Worsboro' Dale, Barnsley, commemorated at Le Touret Memorial, Panel 31

Lance Corporal 9273 Robert George Massey, commemorated at Le Touret Memorial, Panel 31

Private 8417 John Robert Moody, aged 29, son of the late Robert and Sarah Moody of Enington Street, Scotswood Road, Newcastle-on-Tyne; husband of Susannah Moody of 37 Glue Terrace, Elswick, commemorated at Le Touret Memorial, Panel 31

Lance Corporal 10868 Harold Oglesby, commemorated at Le Touret Memorial, Panel 31

Lance Corporal 7823 Thomas Price, commemorated at Le Touret Memorial, Panel 31

Sergeant 7171 Arthur Edward Pridmore, aged 31, son of William and Sarah Pridmore of 34 Hunt Street, Netherthorpe, Sheffield, husband of Annie Elizabeth Pridmore of Bishopthorpe, York, commemorated at Le Touret Memorial, Panel 31

Private 7790 Henry Reed, aged 32, son of James and Sarah Reed of 75 Norton Bridge, Pontypridd; husband of Elizabeth Carnation Fardy (formerly Reed) of 90 Norton Bridge, Pontypridd, Glamorganshire, commemorated at Le Touret Memorial, Panel 31

Private 5866 Frank Horatio Robinson, commemorated at Le Touret Memorial, Panel 31

Lance Corporal 8168 Joseph Roebuck, commemorated at Le Touret Memorial, Panel 31

Private 7145 Albert Silverwood, aged 32, husband of Emma Silverwood of 17 Bath Street, York Road, Leeds, commemorated at Le Touret Memorial, Panel 31

Private 6975 Albert Squires, commemorated at Le Touret Memorial, Panel 31

Private 10896 Percy Turner, aged 21, son of the late William and Mary Ann Turner. His brother also fell. Commemorated at Le Touret Memorial, Panel 31

Private 7165 William Henry Willey, aged 31, son of Mr & Mrs Frederick Willey of Bridgend, Glamorgan; husband of Ellen Willey of Bryn Crier House, Pencoed, Bridgend, Glamorgan, buried at Canadian Cemetery No.2 Neuville-St Vaast, Grave number 15.J.22

Appendix 3

21st West Yorkshire Regiment men killed at Rifle Camp on 27 March 1918

Private 24795 Henry Agar, buried at Mindel Trench British Cemetery, St Laurent-Blangy, Grave number D.12

Private 21/271 Willis Bray, aged 28, only son of Fred and Alice Mary Bray of Bradshaw Road, Honley, Huddersfield, buried at Mindel Trench British Cemetery, St Laurent-Blangy, Grave number D.19

Private 53261 Tom Castle, buried at Mindel Trench British Cemetery, St Laurent-Blangy, Grave number D.16

Private 53267 Charles Edward Cocker, buried at Mindel Trench British Cemetery, St Laurent-Blangy, Grave number D.14

Private 57514 James Crombie, buried at Mindel Trench British Cemetery, St Laurent-Blangy, Grave number D.15

Private 24716 Frederick Cecil Duncan, aged 26, son of George and Emily Ardern Duncan of 7 Highcliffe Street, Michael's Lane, Burley Hill, Leeds, buried at Mindel Trench British Cemetery, St Laurent-Blangy, Grave number D.7

Private 57110 Frederick Charles Durant, buried at Mindel Trench British Cemetery, St Laurent-Blangy, Grave number D.22

Private 16/1438 Charles Horace Fawcett, buried at Mindel Trench British Cemetery, St Laurent-Blangy, Grave number D.21

Private 53277 Albert Gordon Firn, aged 19, son of John Alfred and Emily Elizabeth Firn of 2 Massey Row, New Lane, Selby, Yorkshire, buried at Mindel Trench British Cemetery, St Laurent-Blangy, Grave number D.17

Private 21/329 Frank Edward Furness, buried at Mindel Trench British Cemetery, St Laurent-Blangy, Grave number D.10

Private 21/354 Leonard Jackson, aged 27, nephew of Mrs E. Crowther of 4 Maw Street, Hall Lane, Bradford, buried at Mindel Trench British Cemetery, St Laurent-Blangy, Grave number D.20

Private 58493 William Herbert Jones, aged 22, son of Arthur E. and Clara Jones of 8 Laureston Terrace, Douglas, Isle of Man, buried at Mindel Trench British Cemetery, St Laurent-Blangy, Grave number D.18

Private 21/352 James Mercer, aged 21, son of William and Mary Jane Mercer of 132 St Leonard's Road, Girlington, Bradford, buried at Mindel Trench British Cemetery, St Laurent-Blangy, Grave number D.9

Private 21/238 Joseph Robinson, son of Fred Robinson of Wilberforce Street, Laisterdyke, Bradford, buried at Duisans British Cemetery, Etrun, Grave number V.F.23

Private 43478 Robert Spence, formerly 19/1633 Northumberland Fusiliers, buried at Mindel Trench British Cemetery, St Laurent-Blangy, Grave number D.11

Private 57340 William James Wiley, aged 29, son of Enoch and Mary Wiley; husband of Edith Florence Wiley of 51 King Street, Darlaston, Wednesbury, Staffordshire, buried at Mindel Trench British Cemetery, St Laurent-Blangy, Grave number D.8

Appendix 4

21st West Yorkshire Regiment men killed at Rifle Camp on 28 March 1918

Private 40495 Arthur Grey Ellis, aged 35, son of Richard James and Helen Ellis of Leeds; husband of E.M. Milford (formerly Ellis) of 83 Parkfield Mount, Beeston, Leeds, buried at Ste Catherine British Cemetery, Grave number J.4

Private 238167 Percy Harold French, aged 27, son of Grace French of 81 Ashford Road, Eastbourne, and the late David French, buried at Mindel Trench British Cemetery, St Laurent-Blangy, Grave number D.2

Private 238115 Alexandra Gilmour, son of Mr S. Gilmour of Loch Cottage, Lennie, Lanarkshire, buried at Duisans British Cemetery, Etrun, Grave number V.F.20

Lance Sergeant 21/47 Martin Greenwood, buried at Mindel Trench British Cemetery, St Laurent-Blangy, Grave number D.5

Private 19851 Herbert John Lancaster, aged 30, son of George and Harriet Lancaster of Scarborough; husband of Ellen Lancaster of 9 St Mary's Street, Scarborough, buried at Mindel Trench British Cemetery, St Laurent-Blangy, Grave number D.4

Lance Corporal 18/813 George Lockwood, aged 33, son of Benjamin and Martha Ellen Lockwood; husband of Mrs M Lockwood of 33 Back, Birk Street, Leeds Road, Bradford, buried at Hervin Farm British Cemetery, St Laurent-Blangy, Grave number C.19

Corporal 15/628 Frank McCullagh, aged 23, born at Leeds, son of John and Florence McCullagh of H.M. Prison Liverpool, buried at Mindel Trench British Cemetery, St Laurent-Blangy, Grave number D.6

Private 21/286 Wilfred Morgan, buried at Mindel Trench British Cemetery, St Laurent-Blangy, Grave number D.1

Private 52857 Leslie Nuttall, buried at Mindel Trench British Cemetery, St Laurent-Blangy, Grave number D.3

Private 39391 Benjamin Henry Peel, aged 34, born at Leeds, son of George Ellis and Francis Ann Peel; husband of Hetty Peel of 45 Haddon Road, Burley, Leeds, buried at Faubourg d'Amiens Cemetery, Arras, Grave number VI.D.24

Appendix 5

Burngreave Cemetery

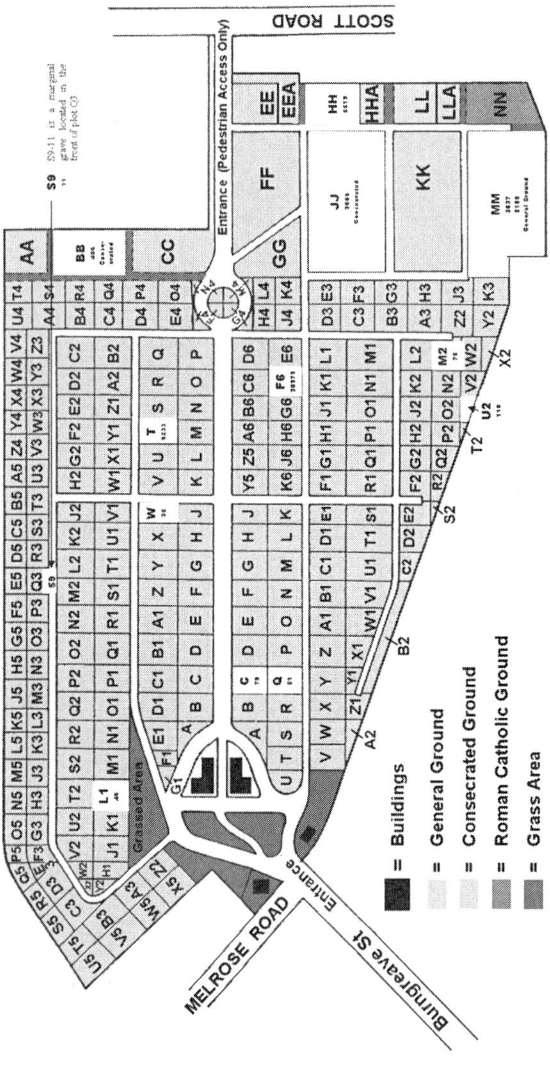

Map courtesy of Friends of Burngreave Chapel and Cemetery adapted by author

Key to Pridmore Graves in Burngreave Cemetery

BB 406 – Lilian May
C 79 – Beatrice Eliza and George Richard Pridmore
HH 5518 – Sarah Jane, William Thomas and Wilfred Pridmore
JJ 3089 – Chloris Pridmore
L1 46 – Stillborn child of Sidney and Catherine Pridmore
M2 75 – Percy Pridmore
MM 2637 – Ernest William and Elizabeth Ann Pridmore
MM 2188 – Philip Pridmore and John Charles May
Q 51 – Ernest and Eliza Pridmore
S9 11 – Charles William May
T 9233 – Mary Theresa and Albert Denis Pridmore
U2 110 – Lily Pridmore
W 35 – Albert Jn., Albert Sen and Margaret Pridmore

Appendix 6

Author's speech at the plaque unveiling, 10 November 2023

My name is Mick Drewry, and I am a great-grandson of John Thomas Pridmore, whose medal ribbons I proudly wear today. I am also responsible for bringing the story of the Pridmore brothers to the attention of the people of Sheffield.

The horrors of war and the futility of war are ever-present on our TV screens and in our newspapers, and we listen to the debates around what constitutes a 'war crime' and what doesn't. Ladies and gentlemen, war itself is a crime against humanity, and war is high-harvest time for the Grim Reaper.

But when we are faced with an aggressor, we must defend ourselves, and throughout history our armed forces have bravely fought to defend Britain and its allies, and throughout history there have been the inevitable casualties, mainly young working-class men killing young working-class men under another flag.

Over time, the war passes beyond living memory, and with the exception of a notable few, the casualties become mere statistics. In the Great War of 1914–1918, some 702,410 British soldiers were recorded as dead or missing. What was not recorded was the number of siblings amongst this tragic figure.

At the time, such information was known only to the families, close friends and their local communities. But with the advent of the internet and an increased interest in genealogy and family history, this information became available to a wider audience.

A number of families across Britain lost five brothers, but here in Sheffield, the greatest loss was that of the Pridmore family, with the loss of the four Pridmore brothers that we are here to commemorate today.

Reaching this point has been quite a journey for me. As a young lad, I was aware that my great-grandfather had been killed in the Great War, as when I visited my grandad, I used to play with his medals and the 'big penny' death plaque that all families received on the loss of a family member during the hostilities – medals that I have inherited and cherish. Grandad didn't tell me much else about his dad, as he was just six years old when John Thomas was killed on 14 October 1914.

Moving the clock forward to around 20 years ago, through a First World War historian I had befriended through my work, I first found that not only was one of my great grandfather's brothers killed just four days after he was - Arthur Edward - but two more brothers also later lost their lives in the conflict – Albert and George Harry.

Naturally, this blew me away and I was determined to raise the profile of the four Pridmore brothers in the hope that they would receive the civic recognition that they truly deserved. At this point, I would like to thank Ben Pridmore for access to his extensive research into the wider Pridmore family, which was most valuable to my own research.

I wrote letters to The Star and a number of articles for their Retro supplement, particularly on relevant anniversaries and Great War centenary commemorations but it wasn't until I wrote directly to Sheffield City Council that my efforts bore fruit and today we are witness to the civic recognition that the Pridmore brothers rightly deserve.

And so, I now want to thank all those involved in the installation of this plaque and in organising today's ceremonies, especially Councillor Denise Fox, who, in recognising the significance of the Pridmore brothers' story, decided to act and took the lead on the project.

I also extend my thanks to Sheffield City Council, East Midlands Rail and Network Rail, who have all contributed to today's very special occasion.

A special thank you to the Deputy Lieutenant for officiating the ceremony.

Also, my sincere thanks for the uniformed presence and support of the Army by way of the Royal Yorkshire Regiment and The Yorkshire Rifles, as well as the support of the KOYLI Museum and the Royal British Legion.

I also thank you, the people of Sheffield, for your attendance today, especially the numerous descendants of the Pridmore brothers and the wider Pridmore family, some of whom I know have travelled a fair distance to be here today.

Before I finish, I would like to let you in on a little secret. The plaque itself was not funded by Sheffield City Council, as you might think. No, it was actually funded by personal donations from four past Masters of the Cutlers' Company in Hallamshire in the County of York. I respect their wish to remain anonymous, but they know who they are, and I am truly grateful for their generosity and their support – four of Sheffield's bravest recognised by four of Sheffield's VIPs.

Thank you – Peace & Love!

Appendix 7

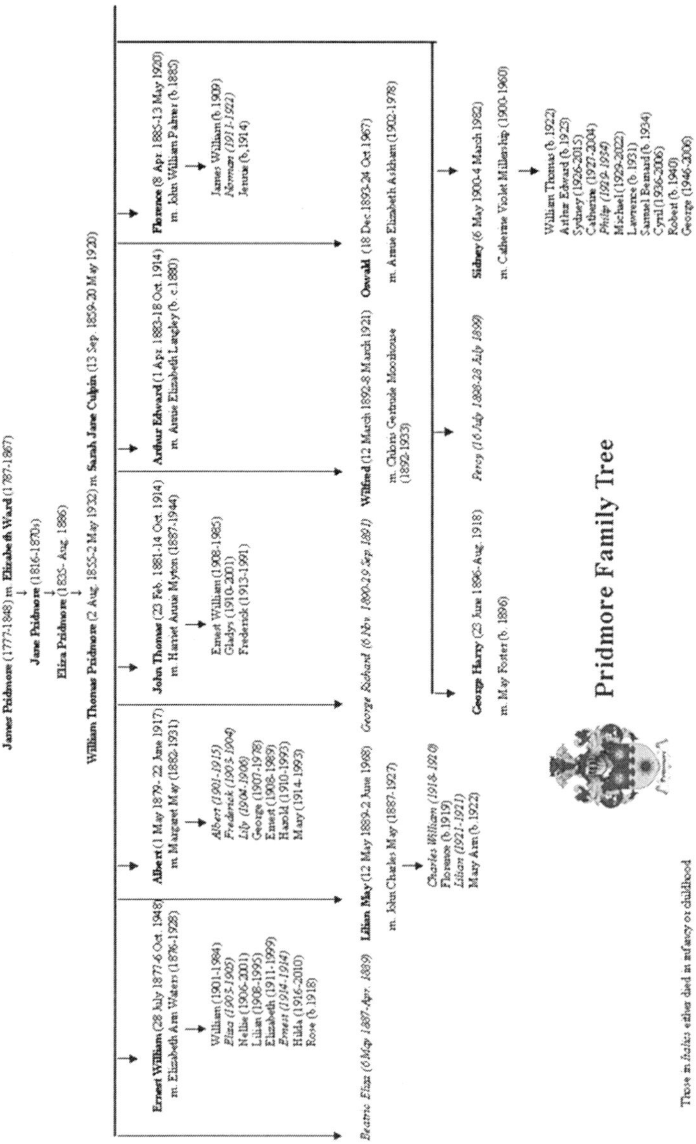

James Pridmore (1777-1848) m. Elizabeth Ward (1787-1867)
Jane Pridmore (1816-1870s)
Eliza Pridmore (1835- Aug. 1886)
William Thomas Pridmore (2 Aug. 1855-2 May 1932) m. Sarah Jane Culpin (13 Sep. 1859-20 May 1920)
Ernest William (28 July 1877-6 Oct. 1948)
m. Elizabeth Ann Waters (1876-1928)
William (1901-1984)
Eliza (1903-1905)
Nellie (1906-2001)
Lilian (1908-1995)
Elizabeth (1911-1999)
Ernest (1914-1914)
Hilda (1916-2010)
Rose (b.1918)
Albert (1 May 1879- 22 June 1917)
m. Margaret May (1882-1931)
Albert (1901-1915)
Frederick (1903-1904)
Lily (1904-1906)
George (1907-1978)
Ernest (1908-1989)
Harold (1910-1993)
Mary (1914-1993)
John Thomas (23 Feb. 1881-14 Oct. 1914)
m. Harriet Annie Myton (1887-1944)
Ernest William (1908-1985)
Gladys (1910-2001)
Frederick (1913-1991)
Arthur Edward (1 Apr. 1883-18 Oct. 1914)
m. Annie Elizabeth Langley (b. c.1880)
Florence (8 Apr. 1885-13 May 1920)
m. John William Palmer (b.1885)
James William (b.1909)
Norman (1911-1922)
Jennie (b.1914)
Beatric Eliza (6 May 1887-Apr. 1889)
Lilian May (12 May 1889-2 June 1968)
m. John Charles May (1887-1927)
Charles William (1918-1920)
Florence (b.1919)
Lilian (1921-1921)
Mary Ann (b.1922)
George Richard (6 Nov. 1890-29 Sep. 1891)
Wilfred (12 March 1892-8 March 1921)
m. Chloris Gertrude Moorhouse
(1892-1933)
Oswald (18 Dec.1893-24 Oct.1967)
m. Annie Elizabeth Askham (1902-1978)
George Harry (23 June 1896-Aug. 1918)
m. May Foster (b. 1896)
Percy (16 July 1898-28 July 1899)
Sidney (6 May 1900-4 March 1982)
m. Catherine Violet Millership (1900-1960)
William Thomas (b.1922)
Arthur Edward (b.1923)
Sydney (1926-2015)
Catherine (1927-2004)
Philip (1929-1934)
Michael (1929-2022)
Lawrence (b.1931)
Samuel Bernard (b.1934)
Cyril (1936-2006)
Robert (b.1940)
George (1946-2006)
Pridmore Family Tree
Those in italics either died in infancy or childhood

Bibliography

Ascoli, David, *Mons Star – The British Expeditionary Force 1914*, Book Club Associates, London, 1981

Beckett, Ian F.W., *Ypres The First Battle 1914*, Routledge, London, 2013

Bond, R.C., *The Kings Own Yorkshire Light Infantry In The Great War – Volume III*, Percy Lund, Humphries & Co Ltd, Bradford

Cassell's *History of the Boer War 1899–1902, Vol. I* Cassell and Company, Limited, London, 1903

Drewry, Mick, *Intimidation – The History, The Times and the People of the Sheffield Outrages*, Austin Macauley Publishers, 2017

Doyle, Peter, *The British Soldier of the First World War,* Shire Publications Ltd, 2014

Eden, Anthony, *Another World*, Penguin Books Ltd, London, 1976

Edmonds, Brigadier-General J.E., *Official History of the Great War – Military Operations France & Belgium 1914, Vol. I,* The Naval & Military Press Ltd and The Imperial War Museum, London

Farwell, Bryon, *The Great Boer War*, Wordsworth Military Library, Wordsworth Edition, Ware, Hertfordshire, 1999

Hetherington, Andrea, *British Widows of the First World War – The Forgotten Legion*, Pen & Sword Military, Barnsley, 2018

Holmes, Richard, *Tommy – The British Soldier on the Western Front 1914–1918,* Harper Collins Publishers, London, 2004

Lewis-Sempell, John, *Six Weeks – The Short and Gallant Life of the British Officer in the First World War,* Weidenfeld & Nicolson, 2010

Lomax, Scott, *The Home Front – Sheffield in the First World War,* Pen & Sword Military, Barnsley, 2014

Murland, Jerry, *Retreat and Rearguard 1914 – The BEF's Actions from Mons to the Marne*, Pen & Sword Military, 2014

Neillands, Robin, *The Old Contemptibles – The British Expeditionary Force, 1914*, John Murray, London, 2004
Nicholls, Jonathon, *Cheerful Sacrifice – The Battle of Arras 1917*, Pen & Sword Military, Barnsley, 2015
Pakenham, Thomas, *The Boer War*, Weidenfeld and Nicolson, London, 1979
Soldiers Died in the Great War 1914–19 – The King's Own (Yorkshire Light Infantry), originally published by the War Office in 1921, my edition published by J.B. Howard & Son in association with The Imperial War Museum Department of Printed Books, 1989
Warr, Peter, *Sheffield in the Great War,* Pen & Sword Military, Barnsley, 2015
Whyte, Wolmer (Ed.), *The Roll of the Drum Histories of the Regiments of the British Army – The King's Own Yorkshire Light Infantry (K. O. Y. L. I. S.),* Hutchinson & Co (Publishers) Ltd, London, 1940
Wyrall, Everard, *The West Yorkshire regiment in the War 1914–1918, Volume Two*, The Naval & Military Press
Other sources:
1881 Census
1891 Census
angloboerwar.com/forum
https://www.britishbattles.com/first-world-war/battle-of-le-cateau/
http://family.nikellom.com/g2/p1195.htm#i29870
https://frankcrawshaw.uk/tag/pont-fixe/
https://www.greatwarforum.org/
The Guardian, 3 November 2003

https://historywm.com/films/hidden-home-front-war-widows-pensions-episode-7

longlongtrail.co.uk/army/regiments-and-corps/the-british-infantry-regiments-of-1914-1918/York-lancaster-regiment/

westernfrontassociation.com/world-war-i-articles/brothers-killed-in-action-together
westernfrontassociation.com/world-war-i-articles/queen-victoria-s-last-vc/
White's Directory of Sheffield and Rotherham, 1911, Kelly's Directories Ltd, Sheffield
National Archives, WO 100/194

National Army Museum website: 1914: To arms, nam.ac.uk/explore/to-arms1914
Queen's Regulations for the Army
Sheffield Daily Independent, Thursday 14 October 1915
Sheffield Daily Telegraph, 24 August 1917
http://www.sheffieldindexers.com/ParishBaptismIndex.html
The Sheffield Star, 21 June 2023
Todd, Nicolas, *The Epidemiological Consequences of War*, video lecture on ultv.univ-lorraine.fr

www.statista.com/statistics/281501/infant-mortality-rate-in-the-united-kingdom/

www.thepastisaforeignpantry.com
Yorkshire Telegraph and Star, 23 August 1917

Also by the author:

The Complete Hillsborough By Her People (Editor), Hillsborough Community Development Trust, 2006

Inundation – The History, The Times And The People of the Great Sheffield Flood Of 1864, YouBooks.co.uk, 2014

Intimidation – The History, The Times And The People Of The Sheffield Outrages, Austin Macauley Publishers, 2017

Insurrection – The History, The Times And The People Of The Sheffield Riots and Risings Of The 18th And 19th Centuries, Austin Macauley Publishers, 2022